Lily's Dream

Praise for the 'Lissadell' series

'A thoroughly enjoyable read and sure to become
a favourite in Irish households.'
Children's Books Ireland

'This historical setting, giving an insight into social-class
division, makes the Lissadell series among her most
accomplished yet.'

Evening Echo

Dedication
For Dan, Brian, Ellen and Annie.

Other Books by Judi Curtin

The Lissadell series
Lily at Lissadell
Lily Steps Up

The 'Molly & Beth' series
Time After Time
Stand By Me
You've Got A Friend

The 'Alice & Megan' series
Alice Next Door
Alice Again
Don't Ask Alice
Alice in the Middle
Bonjour Alice
Alice & Megan Forever
Alice to the Rescue
Viva Alice!
Alice & Megan's Cookbook

The 'Eva' Series
Eva's Journey
Eva's Holiday
Leave it to Eva
Eva and the Hidden Diary
Only Eva

See If Care (with Róisín Meaney)

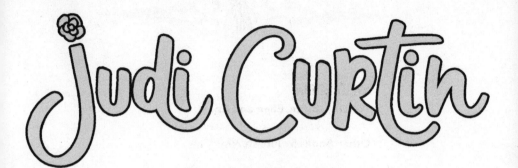

Judi Curtin

Lily's Dream

A Lissadell Story

THE O'BRIEN PRESS
DUBLIN

This edition first published in 2021 by
The O'Brien Press Ltd,
12 Terenure Road East, Rathgar,
Dublin 6, D06 HD27 Ireland.

Tel: +353 1 4923333; Fax: +353 1 4922777

E-mail: books@obrien.ie
Website: www.obrien.ie

The O'Brien Press is a member of Publishing Ireland
ISBN: 978-1-78849-280-5
Text © copyright Judi Curtin 2021

1 3 5 7 8 6 4 2
21 23 24 22

Internal illustration, cover design and cover illustration by Rachel Corcoran.
Internal design by Emma Byrne.
Printed and bound by Norhaven Paperback A/S, Denmark.
The paper in this book is produced using pulp from managed forests.

Published in

DUBLIN
UNESCO
City of Literature

Chapter One

'Hurry up, Lily,' said Maeve, as she pulled off her pretty silk shoes, hitched up her dress and ran towards the sea. 'I bet the water's beautiful.'

'Wait for me,' I said. 'There's a knot in my laces.' Finally I managed to struggle out of my heavy leather boots, and laid them on the sand. Next to Maeve's shoes they looked old and ugly, and for a second I felt ashamed. Then I lifted my head high and told myself I was being foolish. I had a good honest job at Lissadell, and just because I was a servant, and Maeve was a member of the family who owned the house, that didn't make her better than me.

I took a second to enjoy the feeling of the warm sand under my feet, then I pulled off my housemaid's cap and ran to the water, to my friend, to the best moments of my day.

'I wish I'd brought my swimming costume, don't you?' said Maeve as we paddled.

'I don't have one. Years ago, before my daddy died, he took my whole family to Rosses Point for a day, and Mam let me wear an old petticoat of hers to swim in. I'm too big for that kind of thing now though.'

'Oh,' said Maeve, looking embarrassed. 'I've got two costumes – you can borrow one next time if you like.'

'Thank you.' Maeve was always generous.

It was a gorgeous sunny day. A gentle breeze tossed my hair, and a flock of seagulls screeched and squawked over our heads while Maeve and I chatted.

'Tell me the news of your sisters,' she said.

Maeve loved hearing stories about Winnie and Anne, even though she had her own sweet cousins

at Lissadell – Michael, Hugh, Bridget, Brian and little baby Rosaleen. She laughed when I told her how Winnie was afraid of the tiny little puppy who strayed into our garden one day.

'Oh, how I love the sea,' I sighed, as the water rippled over my skin. 'When I'm a teacher, I'm going to work by the seaside, and every single day I'll go for a paddle after school, even if I'm very old like twenty-five or something.'

'When *I* grow up, I'm going to live in Dublin,' said Maeve. 'So I can be near Mother. The two of us will take trips to the seaside, and we shall be so happy together.'

'That sounds lovely.'

Maeve's mam lived in Dublin, and her daddy was somewhere in Europe, and I knew she missed them very much. Now she lived at Ardeevin with her grandmother, Gaga, but she spent lots of time at Lissadell House with her Uncle Josslyn and Aunt Mary and their children. She had many good things

in her life, but I knew she was often lonely.

We paddled until our toes went white from the cold. Then we sat on a rock, and we each used one of my stockings to dry our feet.

We walked along the path, away from the sea. As always, I stopped for a moment and looked at Lissadell House – so dark and huge. I remembered the first time I'd seen it, almost a year earlier. Back then I was so young and scared, but now I marched towards it, a little older, and not scared any more.

'Now what will we do?' asked Maeve as we walked. 'Maybe Albert could take us for a drive? Or we could go to my room and play dress-up, or we could...'

'I'd love to do both of those things, but I can't. I should have been back at work ages ago, and if I don't hurry up, Mrs Bailey will make a fuss.'

It didn't matter how nice the weather was – I wasn't supposed to be on the beach in the middle of the afternoon. I was supposed to be helping my friend Nellie to clean the drawing room. When Maeve and

I first became friends, she used to tell the house-keeper that she needed me to pose for a painting – which wasn't really true at all. I'm not sure if Mrs Bailey ever believed her, but the servants felt sorry for Maeve, so she never made a fuss. Nowadays, Maeve didn't even bother to pretend – she just showed up and smiled and Mrs Bailey would shake her head at me and warn me not to be away for too long.

'Sorry, Lily,' said Maeve. 'I forgot you had to go back to work. Are you very cross with me?'

I *had* been cross with her, but now she was smiling so sweetly, I couldn't keep it up.

'No,' I said.

'So we're still friends?'

'Of course we are. Always!'

Now she smiled even more. She took my hand and together we skipped along the path.

* * *

I managed to avoid Mrs Bailey as I gathered my mop

and bucket and hurried to the drawing room. Nellie was on her knees dusting under the dresser, but she looked up and smiled when she saw me.

'Did you have a nice time with Maeve? Was the water very cold? Have you got sand in your stockings? I really hate that.'

I smiled back at her, realising how lucky I was to have Nellie as a friend. Other girls would feel jealous of my friendship with Maeve, and resent having to start on the rooms without me. Nellie wasn't like that though. She always wanted me to have a nice time.

'It was lovely,' I said as I knelt down beside her and began to work. 'The water was a little bit cold, but—'

Just then Lady Mary came into the room. Nellie and I put down our dusters and stood with our hands clasped in front of us, the way we had been taught.

'Ah, there you are, Lily,' said Lady Mary. 'I was wondering how you are getting along with your little project for the Home Industries show? Didn't you say you are going to make a blouse for your mother?'

I put my head down. Lady Mary was very kind. She always asked about my family and encouraged me with my sewing.

'I ... I haven't got started on it yet, Lady Mary,' I said.

'Why ever not?' she said. 'The show isn't too far away now, and if you do your best work, I'm sure you have a very good chance of winning a prize.'

'I ...'

'Had you forgotten all about it?'

'No ... it's just that ...'

How could I begin to explain to this fine lady?

How could she ever understand my life?

Of course I haven't forgotten about the home industries show – the prize for the best garment is three whole shillings! If I had three shillings, I'd buy cream for Mam's sore hands – and maybe I could get some ribbons for my little sisters, and a few marbles for my brothers. But where am I supposed to find the time to sew that perfect garment? Mrs Bailey has me working all the hours – when Nellie

and I get to bed, we're usually asleep within minutes – on Friday I'm in the sewing school and on Saturdays when it's my day off I travel home to see Mam and help her with jobs – and Maeve is always asking me to spend time with her, and I like that but it doesn't leave me with much time for sewing and...

'Well?' Lady Mary didn't look cross – she looked disappointed, which was far worse. But then, as she stared at me, it was almost as if she understood.

'I know you work very hard, Lily,' she said gently. 'But if you can find the time at all, don't forget you can take fabric and whatever else you need from the cupboard under the attic stairs.'

'Thank you, Lady Mary,' I said. 'You're very kind.'

* * *

That evening, Nellie came with me as I went to the fabric cupboard.

'Oh my!' she said when I opened the door. 'This is

a real treasure trove. You're so lucky, Lily.'

'Would you like to sew something too?' I said. 'I'm sure Lady Mary would let you...'

'Not me,' she laughed. 'My stitches aren't neat like yours. I can mend sheets, but that's about all. If I put something in the Home Industries show I'd be the laugh of the whole estate.'

'If anyone laughs at you, I'll thump them,' I said, but I didn't argue. Nellie had many great talents, but sewing wasn't one of them.

The two of us leaned in and touched the stacks of fabric – so soft and cool under our fingers.

'This pink one,' said Nellie. 'No this green one – or maybe the yellow one with the stripes. What's your Mam's favourite colour?'

'She likes blue,' I said, reaching in and pulling out a piece of cotton. We each took two corners and held the fabric out to the light. It was fine and soft and the colour of the sky on the best day of the year.

'That's the one,' sighed Nellie. 'It's beautiful.'

'You're right,' I said. 'I can put a small frill on the neck, and puff out the sleeves, like on Lady Mary's blouses. Mam won't like anything too fancy, but I think I could get away with a few little things.'

As we folded the fabric and went downstairs for our supper, I couldn't help feeling excited. I *was* going to make the blouse. I *was* going to win the home industries show. And Mam was going to be the finest lady in our village!

Chapter Two

The door to the little room off the kitchen was open, and I slipped inside. Harry, one of the footmen, was ironing the newspapers.

'Hello, Lily,' he said. 'How are you today? Are you a teacher yet?'

'Not quite yet,' I said, laughing. 'Maybe next week.'

Harry, like all my friends, knew that my great ambition was to be a teacher. Sometimes I feared this would never happen, but Harry always encouraged me. Harry always believed in me.

'I've been wondering why you iron the papers.' I said. 'They're barely wrinkled at all.'

'It's not only about the wrinkles,' he said. 'The iron dries the ink too, so Sir Josslyn doesn't get his fingers dirty.'

'It's a lot of work for you, though,' I said.

'True – but I don't mind – and anyway, it means I can keep up with all the latest news.'

'What's happening out there?'

Now his face went serious. 'It's not good, Lily. Not good at all.'

'Is it Countess Markievicz again?'

Maeve's mother, Countess Markievicz, was always getting into trouble. She was often mentioned in the newspaper for going on marches, and some of the servants said that once she was even arrested!

'No, it's not the Countess,' he said. 'There's bad things happening in Europe, Lily.'

'Like what?' his serious face was making me nervous.

'Remember I told you about Archduke Franz Ferdinand being shot?'

I did. I felt sorry for the man – being shot can't be very nice – but I still couldn't see why that mattered to me. People on our own island were dying all the time.

'But I'd never even heard of him,' I said. 'Or the place he was shot. Is it still in the newspapers?'

'Well, it's complicated to explain, but that set off a series of events, and now things are very tense in Germany and Russia. There could be a war coming.'

'War isn't nice – but Germany and Russia are so far away – how will that make any difference to us here at Lissadell?'

'If Great Britain gets involved, it could change life here too.'

'And do you think that will happen?'

'The Irish Volunteers will be a distraction, but who knows?'

I listened to adults talking all the time so I knew that lots of people believed Ireland should be free. I knew lots of people were prepared to fight for that freedom, but this talk of war with other countries was very frightening.

'Ah, now, Lily,' said Harry. 'I shouldn't be making you worry. I'm sure it will all blow over soon.

Nobody wants...'

I heard footsteps in the passageway behind me, but I knew it wasn't the firm march of Mrs Bailey's feet, so I didn't bother to turn around. Then I noticed that Harry's face had gone red.

'Who was that?' I asked. 'And why are you smiling?'

'No one,' he said, still smiling that funny smile.

Now I was really interested, but when I peeped out, there was no one to be seen.

'Harry?' I said, but now his blush had faded, and he was busy ironing the last page of the last newspaper.

'Time for me to go,' he said, putting the iron down. 'Sir Josslyn won't be happy if the papers are out of date before I get them upstairs.'

'Harry?' I said again, but he gathered up the newspapers, winked, and walked around me and out the door. Very strange.

* * *

My room was in the basement of the house. It was small with just two beds, two lockers and a press. It was cosy though, with a gas light, and a fireplace for cold winter nights. Nellie was in bed reading when I got there that night.

'At last I've got all the pieces for Mam's blouse cut out,' I said. 'It took much longer than I expected.'

'It's going to be lovely,' she said.

'It had better be – as everyone's being so helpful. Mrs Bailey let me use the servant's dining table for the cutting, Lady Mary gave me thread and needles and buttons, and Johanna gave me this lovely cotton bag to keep everything in.'

At the mention of her sister's name, Nellie looked up and smiled. They had once been in a workhouse, and lost track of each other for many years. Lady Mary, Maeve and I helped to bring them together, and now Johanna worked as a lady's maid at Lissadell.

'Is it all right if I sew for a few minutes before putting out the light?' I asked. 'I'm keen to get started.'

'Of course.'

I took out the first two pieces, threaded my needle and began to sew, using my best, tiniest stitches. I loved starting a new project, and felt I could sew all through the night. But Nellie and I had been up since six that morning, and before long we were yawning so much we had tears in our eyes. I put my sewing away, turned out the gas light, and was asleep in seconds.

* * *

Next day, Nellie and I were told to mend sheets, so we hurried along to the bright sunny room where we did the darning and other small jobs like that. I loved sewing, and it was a chance to sit down and chat, but poor Nellie wasn't so happy.

'Ouch!' she said after only a few minutes. 'I've stabbed myself again. These needles are dangerous weapons.'

Just then Johanna came in and sat beside her sister.

'You poor girl,' she petted. 'Is it bad?'

Nellie beamed. She didn't care about pain when her beloved big sister was next to her, taking care of her.

Johanna was a few years older than Nellie and me, and sometimes she seemed like a real grown-up. She was funny, and always made Nellie and me laugh over silly things. When Johanna first came to Lissadell, I didn't like her, but now all that had changed, and I loved her like a sister.

'Can you sit with us for a few minutes, Johanna?' asked Nellie.

'I can sit with you for lots of minutes,' smiled Johanna, opening the leather case she was carrying. 'Lady Mary has asked me to polish her jewellery, and it's going to take me ages.'

The three of us worked away, chatting about this and that. Then I remembered my conversation with Harry.

'When I was in the dining room I heard Sir Joss-

lyn and Lady Mary talking,' said Nellie, when I'd told them what Harry had said. 'They are worried too. I don't like hearing about wars and things like that – it frightens me.'

'It *is* scary,' said Johanna. 'But Harry is right to tell us. We should know what's going on in the outside world.'

Something in Johanna's voice made me look up. Was she blushing? Why was she smiling while talking about war?

I put down my sewing and watched her, trying to work out what was going on – and then I understood.

'Johanna?' I said.

'What?'

'Why has your face turned that pretty shade of pink?'

'I don't know what you're talking about,' she said, turning even pinker than before.

'Lily's right,' said Nellie. 'You *are* pink – are you all right?'

'It's a little warm in here,' said Johanna.

I laughed. 'That's not it. Nellie and I are as pale as we ever were.'

'Maybe I have a touch of fever,' said Johanna.

'Maybe you have,' I laughed. 'But I think that fever got worse when I mentioned Harry's name.'

'Johanna!' said Nellie. 'Are you and Harry...?'

'Don't be silly,' said Johanna. 'Harry and I sometimes chat together, that's all. He's interesting, and I like to hear what he says about the news.'

Nellie looked as if she believed her sister, but I wasn't so sure. Mam often tells me that you can't always believe the words people say, but their eyes can't lie. Johanna's eyes were sparkling, and telling me that there was *definitely* something going on between her and Harry. I wondered if Nellie would mind – her sister had been lost to her for so long, would she be sorry to share her now?

'How's your mam's blouse coming along, Lily?' asked Johanna. 'It's going to be lovely when it's

finished.'

I smiled, pretending I hadn't noticed the way she changed the subject so quickly. Life at Lissadell House was boring sometimes, and a little bit of romance would be a nice distraction.

Chapter Three

Sometimes on Sundays, when there were no guests at the house, we were allowed to have two hours off in the afternoon. Servants at Lissadell worked hard, and this was a special treat.

After dinner, Nellie, Johanna and I left the servants' dining hall together.

'Two whole hours,' sighed Nellie. 'What are you going to do, Lily?'

'I'm going to work on Mam's blouse – I want to get lots done.'

Nellie turned to her sister. 'Johanna, maybe you and I could...?'

Before she could finish, Harry came over. Once again his face was pink, and when Johanna saw him, her face turned a matching colour.

'Johanna?' he said. 'I wonder if, if... what I mean

is... would you...?'

Watching him was funny, but I felt sorry for him too. Harry was always so confident, and now he was like a little schoolboy, in trouble for not doing his homework.

He tried again. 'Johanna. I wonder if maybe you would like to...?'

I knew I'd have to help him. 'Harry,' I said. 'We only have two hours off, and at this rate, you're going to spend the whole time here in this passageway, not able to get to the end of your sentence.'

Nellie giggled, and Johanna poked me with her elbow, but I ignored her. I was only trying to help.

'Just spit it out,' I said. 'It sounds as if you want to ask Johanna to do something with you?'

Harry nodded, his face now almost purple. He opened his mouth, but no words came out.

'So what do you want to do?' I asked. With only two hours, there really weren't many options. 'Walk into the village? Walk around the garden? Walk

along the beach?'

He nodded again, and I turned to Johanna. 'It looks as if Harry wants to go for a walk on the beach with you.'

She still looked embarrassed, but she also had a huge smile on her face. She was so happy, and so beautiful, I wanted to throw my arms around her and give her a huge hug – but everyone was awkward enough already, so I stopped myself.

'I'd like that, thank you, Harry,' she said. Now he too looked as if he'd been given the best present in the world, before Johanna spoke again. 'Oh, Nellie,' she said. 'You were going to say something. Did you want to...?'

And kind Nellie, whose favourite thing in the world was spending time with her sister, shook her head. 'Oh, I was only going to ask ... if you wanted to ... come to our room tonight, so we could read together.'

'Why don't you come for a walk with Johanna and

me, Nellie?' said Harry, showing what a nice person
he was. 'And you too, Lily.'

'Thank you,' I said. 'But I'm going to my room to
do my sewing.'

'And I'm going with you, Lily,' said Nellie. 'I'll sing
to you while you work.'

And so Nellie and I went to our room, leaving
Johanna and Harry to their romantic walk on the
beach.

* * *

After our break, we had lots of work to do, so Nellie
and I didn't see Johanna. It was late that evening and
we were already in bed when Johanna finally came to
our room. She took off her shoes and slipped under
the covers with her sister.

'Tell us everything,' I said sitting up. 'I want to hear
every single detail.'

'There's nothing to tell,' said Johanna primly. 'Harry
and I had a lovely walk, and then we came back, and

I've been helping Lady Mary to sort out her wardrobe ever since.'

'What did you and Harry talk about?' asked Nellie.

'All kinds of things,' sighed Johanna, with a small smile on her face. 'We talked about his brother in England, and his daddy's farm, and what's happening in Europe. And sometimes we didn't talk at all – and that didn't matter – we only walked along – and it was lovely.'

'And will you and Harry go walking again?' I asked.

'We might,' said Johanna. 'If you don't mind, Nellie?'

'Why would I mind?' asked Nellie.

'Because – well ... because if I'm with Harry, then I'm not with you, and I don't want you to be lonely.'

'I was lonely when I didn't know where you were, or even if you were alive. Now you're here with me, and I don't mind if you want to spend time with Harry.'

'If you're sure?' said Johanna.

'Of course I'm sure,' said Nellie. 'All I want is for

you to be happy.'

Johanna kissed her little sister, then she tiptoed from the room, and we settled down to sleep.

* * *

After that, Harry and Johanna went on lots of walks. Soon they didn't get all red and embarrassed when they were together – they just looked happy. I noticed that when one was talking, the other paid extra attention to what they were saying, as if their words were more valuable than anyone else's. Watching them reminded me a bit of how my mam and daddy used to be, and it made me sad and happy at the same time.

Chapter Four

*N*ellie and I had to clean the butler's office. Mr Kilgallon was very fussy about his things, and we were both a little bit scared of him, so we took a long time, making sure to put everything carefully back in its place.

'I wonder what's for dinner?' said Nellie as we put our mops and buckets back in the store room. 'I'm so hungry I think I might die if I don't get it soon.'

I peeped around the door at the kitchen clock. 'Please don't die,' I said. 'You've only got ten minutes to wait.'

She laughed. 'I'm going to take my place at the table right now,' she said. 'In case I suddenly become too weak. Are you coming?'

'No,' I said. 'I'm going to run to our room and spend the ten minutes sewing. The Home Industries

show will be on soon – and every stitch counts.'

As I hurried along the corridor, I bumped into Maeve.

'Oh, Lily,' she said happily. 'I've been looking for you.'

I smiled. I knew she was looking for me, as otherwise she wouldn't have been in the servants' area. Like the rest of her family, she spent most of her time in the beautiful upstairs rooms.

'Do you want to come to the stables to look at the horses?' she asked.

'I'd love to – but I can't.'

'Why not?'

'Dinner is in ten minutes.'

'If we hurry, ten minutes will be enough – well maybe not – but it doesn't matter – I can explain to Mrs Bailey – and Cook can leave your dinner on a tray.'

I didn't know whether to laugh or cry. Did Maeve have any idea what Cook would say if I asked her

to put dinner aside especially for me? Unless there was a huge emergency, everyone had to eat at the correct times, all gathered around the big table in the servants' dining hall. And after dinner, there wouldn't be time for me to eat anyway. Mrs Bailey had lots of jobs for me – enough to keep me going non-stop until teatime.

'I have to eat with the rest of the servants,' I said quietly.

'Well then, we'd better hurry. If we run you can be back in time.'

'But I wanted to spend this ten minutes working on Mam's new blouse – I need to have it finished in time for the Home Industries show.'

'Who cares about the Home Industries show?'

'I do!'

'Why? I don't know why you're making such a fuss about it. It's only a silly old show that's on every year.'

It was easy for Maeve, with her exciting life. She was always doing things that were so much fun.

'It's not silly to me,' I said. 'I want to enter – and I want to win.'

'But why?'

'Back when I was at school, I was the best at writing stories. I loved when the master praised me – and he often read out my story for the whole school. I miss that feeling.'

'I heard Mrs Bailey saying you did a great job polishing the golden birds on the stairs the other day.'

I laughed. 'That's true – but I don't want to be the best at polishing! I want to be the best at something I *like* doing – writing, or sewing, or teaching. And it's not only about that – I want the prize too. It's three whole shillings.'

'Is that all?'

I looked at my friend. How could she *ever* understand? If she wanted three shillings, all she had to do was ask her grandmother, or her uncle or aunt, and they'd give it to her straight away. Life wasn't like that for me. I gave most of my wages to Mam, to help her take care of my little brothers and sisters. Three shillings was a fortune to me.

Maeve often forgot how different my situation was to hers. As a servant, it wasn't so easy for me to forget.

But I didn't want to fight with my friend, so I didn't say any of this.

'I'm sorry I can't go to the stables with you,' I said, as I heard the bell calling the servants to the dining hall. 'I've got to go for my dinner. I'll see you ... well, I'll see you some time soon.'

Maeve looked disappointed, but she didn't notice that I was disappointed too. Didn't she realise how precious that ten minutes of sewing would have been to me?

I walked towards the dining hall, which was buzzing with chatter and laughter and the rattle of plates and cutlery. I liked mealtimes with Nellie, Johanna, Harry and all my other friends, and I couldn't help feeling sorry for Maeve as she went upstairs on her own, with her head down.

* * *

Saturday was my day off, and as usual, I borrowed Maeve's bicycle for the journey to see my family. I was happy, but also worried about what would happen when I got home. Before I went to Lissadell, I didn't keep secrets from Mam, but now things were different. I never told her I was friends with Maeve, because she'd worry that such a friendship would get me into trouble with my employers.

So how could I ask for her advice?

How could I explain that Maeve was a kind girl, but sometimes said cruel things without meaning them, or understanding how they were going to hurt me?

How could I tell Mam I was worried Maeve and I couldn't be friends any more – that we were too different, that we dreamed of different things, that our lives were going to lead us along very different paths?

And when you're trying very hard not to mention something, isn't that the thing that always bursts out of your mouth?

But I shouldn't have worried at all. When I went in, Mam gave me one of her gorgeous big hugs, and called me her darling girl. Winnie and Anne ran to me, fighting over who could cling to my skirt. My brothers, Denis and Jimmy, smiled shyly and came to see what was in the basket Cook had sent.

Mam had washed the children's sheets, and after dinner, while she was weeding the vegetable patch, I went in to make the bed. It seemed small, for four children, and I could hardly imagine any more what it was like when I had to share it too. As I bent to tuck in the bottom sheet, my fingers touched something under the mattress. It was the story I had written in my last week at school! I had hoped I could read it out to the whole class. I had hoped the Master would clap his hands and say what a great little writer I was. But before any of that happened, I had to leave

school and go to work at Lissadell. On the day I left home, I tucked the story under the mattress, hoping that one day I could come back and go to school again, and be with my friends Hanora and Rose, and everything would go back the way it was. But now Rose was living in Sligo, working in her uncle's shop, and Hanora was all the way over in America. None of us was ever going back to our lovely school in the village.

I slid to the floor and began to read the story. It was about three girls who get lost in the woods and find a magical underground world where all their dreams come true. I smiled as I tried to remember the little girl who had written the story. Did she really believe that dreams can come true?

Did I?

'Lily, pet, you're crying. What's the matter, my darling girl?'

Mam dropped the bundle of clothes she was carrying and sat on the floor beside me. She used a clean

hanky to wipe my tears away.

I put the story down and wiped my eyes. 'Oh, Mam,' I said. 'Life was much easier when I was a little girl, and you and Daddy could make everything right.'

'Oh, my darling,' she said. 'I'm sorry you're sad. I'm sorry your daddy isn't with us. I'm sorry you couldn't stay at school. You just have to do your best, and believe that things will turn out well in the end – though it might be different to what you expected.'

For a while we sat on the floor, not talking at all, wrapped up in our own small world. Being there with my lovely mam was enough, and before long I began to feel better.

'Come on, Mam,' I said in the end, jumping up and giving her my hand. 'Let's take the girls for a walk. Let's enjoy our day.'

* * *

The lovely day went too fast, and I managed not to mention Maeve, or Mam's new blouse or the Home Industries show, and before I knew it I was back at Lissadell, saying good-night to Nellie, and settling down in my little iron bed.

Chapter Five

'What's the news?' I asked Harry the next day when I passed him on the servants' staircase.

'Not good,' he said. 'Not good at all. Germany has declared war on France, and invaded Belgium.'

'I'm sorry to hear that,' I said, though I wasn't sure why he was so upset. Harry had been reading me bits from the papers for months now, and there always seemed to be a war somewhere far away. Why was this one so different?

'Do you want to know why this matters?' he asked, as if he could read my mind.

I nodded.

'Belgium is a small, Catholic country, just like us. The world can't stand by and watch as the Belgian people suffer. I don't like saying this, but I think it's only a matter of time before we become

part of this war.'

'And will Irish people really go to fight?'

'Probably. Some will go because they believe in the cause, but there are all kinds of reasons for men to go to war.'

'Like what?'

'You and I have good jobs, but not everyone is so lucky. Some men will join up for the money – army pay isn't bad, and there's even a chance of a pension afterwards. And some poor lads will join up thinking it's all a big adventure – and by the time they realise the truth, it's too late to change their minds. War is a bad business, Lily.'

I didn't like thinking about such sad things so I continued up the stairs, telling myself that it would probably never happen.

* * *

Next morning, when I was sent to clear away the

breakfast things from the dining room, Sir Josslyn and Lady Mary were still there. They looked very serious and didn't take any notice of me as I began to gather the dishes and stack them on the sideboard.

'I can barely believe this is happening,' Sir Josslyn said, as he turned a page of his newspaper.

What? I wanted to ask, but of course I was not allowed to join in with family conversations. Luckily he continued speaking, as I very slowly removed the serving dishes and spoons from the table. I moved them around for a bit on the sideboard, trying to look busy.

'For the Prime Minister to declare war on Germany like that!' he continued. 'Surely there were ways this could have been avoided.'

Lady Mary patted his arm, but didn't reply.

Sir Josslyn continued to read. 'It says that when war was declared, crowds gathered outside Buckingham Palace, waving their hats and cheering. The King and Queen came out to the balcony several times, and

everyone sang the national anthem. Just look at this photo, Mary!'

Lady Mary leaned over and stared at the picture, with a shocked look on her face. I wanted to see it too, but by the time I thought to pick up the teapot and go over to Sir Josslyn, he had turned the page.

It all sounded very exciting to me – like a big party. I wondered what it would be like to stand outside a palace, to see a real king and queen with my very own eyes – but I felt bad when Sir Josslyn gave a big sigh.

'Britain has to do the right thing – but this celebration is beyond belief. Don't people read history books? War is not a pleasant business, and the sooner this one is over, the better.'

He turned another page, and shook his head.

'Already,' he said. 'It's happening already.'

'What is it, my dear?' asked Lady Mary.

'There has been an attack on a German butcher's shop in London – all the windows were smashed and the place was destroyed. Some poor man trying to

make a living – and for this to happen simply because of where he was born...'

I wanted to hear more, but Lady Mary was looking at me, probably wondering why I was still there.

'Can I get you anything else, Lady Mary?' I asked.

'No thank you, Lily,' she said. 'You may leave us.'

I left the room as slowly as I could. I even dropped a few things, and took my time picking them up, but Sir Josslyn didn't say any more.

On my way across the hall I met Maeve.

'There's going to be a war,' I said. 'Have you heard?'

'Yes. Uncle Josslyn told me – but that won't make much of a difference to us. Nothing ever happens here – and I don't expect that will change.'

I wanted to believe her, but wasn't sure I could.

'Where are you going?' I asked, noticing that she was wearing a hat and a lovely light summer coat.

'Oh, Albert is taking me back to Ardeevin. Grandmother says I can't miss any more lessons with Miss Clayton, and if I make a fuss, Mother will get

involved and threaten to send me to boarding school in England again.'

'When will you be back?' I asked.

'Who knows when I'll be able to escape from my evil governess?'

I smiled, but it wasn't a real smile. Miss Clayton wasn't at all evil, and I was half-jealous of Maeve. I'd have loved a world where I could have any kind of schooling at all.

We heard the horn of the motor car beeping.

'Have to go. See you, Lily,' said Maeve.

I felt sad as she closed the front door behind her. Maeve and I didn't always agree, but life was much more interesting when she was around.

* * *

Next morning I hummed to myself as I crossed the courtyard. Except for my day off, Friday was my favourite day of the week – the day I spent helping

Miss Connor in the needlework school. Sometimes I could hardly believe my luck – being allowed to spend a whole day teaching sewing, without a mop or a duster anywhere in sight. As I went upstairs, I was surprised that no one was singing. A few of the women had lovely voices, and there was nearly always someone keen to share a new song. When I got inside though, huddles of women were whispering together, looking serious. As I walked to the table where my usual group of five was sitting, I heard the word 'war' repeated over and over. Mary-Kate, the woman I liked best, patted my hand as I sat down.

'Isn't it terrible news altogether about the war?' she said.

'It is,' I said, still not sure how it was going to affect my life. There had been a bit of talk in the servants' dining hall the evening before, but Mr Kilgallon put a stop to it when Ita, the scullery maid, started to cry.

'I always wanted a son,' said Mary-Kate. 'I dreamed of a fine boy to help his dad in the fields, and now I

thank my lucky stars that I only had my seven girls.'

She saw the confused look on my face. 'Girls can't go to war,' she said.

'You mean Irish boys will really be going away to fight?' This is what Harry had told me, but I was still hoping he'd been wrong.

'Of course they will. Poor Lizzie Mangan over there has five strapping sons.'

I looked across the room at Lizzie, and saw that the usually laughing woman was sewing quietly, with a grim look on her face.

'The four oldest boys are already planning to sign up,' said Mary-Kate. 'And though the youngest is only fifteen, he's threatening to lie about his age, and go too. Lizzie says she'll beat him if he does, but if he goes behind her back, there's nothing she can do.'

'Poor Lizzie,' I said, realising for the first time how this war might come to Lissadell.

As Mary-Kate pointed out all the other women who had sons, I said a quiet prayer of thanks that my

own two brothers were only ten and eleven. The very thought of my darling Denis and Jimmy marching off to war brought tears to my eyes.

Just then Mrs Connor walked past, and I remembered that I was supposed to be working. I picked up a needle and thread and began to sew, demonstrating a new lace stitch.

Teaching in the sewing school was strange, as all my pupils were so much older than me – and some were even older than Mam! I loved my work, but this wasn't my dream. One day I was going to teach little children, helping them to read and write and do sums. One day.

'Lily, I'm stuck on this bit. Can you show me again?' Mary-Kate interrupted my daydream.

'Of course,' I said, holding out my own work. 'Hold the needle like this, and turn the fabric. Yes, that's the way. Well done!'

She smiled at me, delighted with herself, and I felt a sudden rush of happiness. The sewing school wasn't

my dream, but I was learning how to be a teacher, and it was one more step on my journey.

* * *

After lunch, Miss Connor clapped her hands, and the room fell quiet. 'Anyone who is entering the Home Industries show can take out their work now,' she said.

She had told us the week before that this would be allowed, so now nearly everyone put away their school work, and took out their own projects. There were lots of categories in the competition, and everyone seemed to have chosen a different one. A busy chatter spread across the room, as we admired each other's work.

I shyly took out Mam's blouse, which was at last starting to take shape.

'Oh,' said Mary-Kate when she saw it. 'It's simply perfect. It's lucky no one else here is making a blouse

for the competition, as they'd surely be wasting their time.'

The other women nodded and sighed as they too admired my work.

Mary-Kate held up the tiny white dress she was making for her grand-daughter. 'I have no hope of winning,' she said. 'But sure it's a bit of fun – and at the end little Doris will have her own new dress.'

'It's beautiful,' I said. 'And it could easily win. You sew so well now.'

I took some pride in saying this. When I started to teach Mary-Kate, her stitches had been big and rough, but now they were almost as good as mine.

She beamed at me. She was many years older than me, but because I was her teacher, she respected my words.

'Ah, now,' she said shyly. 'You're only saying that – I know I have no chance at all, at all.'

I'd never been to the Home Industries show before and didn't know how high the standard was. Sud-

denly, I wished that Mary-Kate would win – almost as much as I wished it for myself.

I admired the other women's sewing – an embroidered handkerchief, a night-dress, a lace collar and a man's shirt, and then we all settled down to our work. Soon, as we concentrated on our sewing, a happy, buzzy feeling came across the room. Maybe, far away in Europe, men were already fighting and dying, but it's funny how you can forget big important things like war, when your mind is on small things like the next stitch, and the next stitch and the one after that.

Chapter Six

'**G**oodbye, darling Lily. Safe travels home, and we'll see you next Saturday.'

Mam gave me a hug, while my little sisters jumped up and down beside us. Inside the house, my brothers were acting as if they didn't care if I was there or not – I didn't mind as I knew they were only pretending. I'd had a lovely day with my family, but now the moment I'd been dreading was here.

'Actually, Mam, I can't come home next Saturday,' I said.

'Oh,' said Mam. 'What day will you be coming then?'

'I can't come any day. Saturday is still my day off, but there's this show at Lissadell – and I want to go.'

'What kind of show?'

'It's called the Home Industries show. People enter

pots of flowers and vegetables, and sewing and lace and things like that. There's prizes, and the other servants say it's a lovely day.'

'And are you entering one of the competitions?'

'Oh, maybe … I'll see if I get time to make something.' (The blouse was still a *big* secret.)

'Well, you're talented with the needle, so if you make something, I'm sure it will be the best. And if you don't, I hope you have a lovely day with all your new friends.'

'So you don't mind me not coming home?'

Mam patted my arm, and once again I noticed how red and sore her hands were. I *had* to win the prize, and buy her the special cream.

'My sweet girl,' she said. 'We'll miss you, but we'll get over it, and when we see you in two weeks' time, we'll be happier than we ever were. Now up you get on your bike and off you go before it gets dark.'

'I love you, Mam,' I said. Then I kissed my sisters, called goodbye to my brothers, and set off back to Lissadell.

'Finished at last!' I said. 'Just in time for the show tomorrow.' I cut off the thread, put down my needle and laid the blouse flat on my bed.

'Oh, Lily,' said Nellie, coming over for a look. 'That is ... I can hardly find the words ... it is so ... so, so beautiful.'

'Thank you, dear Nellie,' I said. I didn't want to sound vain by agreeing with her, but the fact is, I was very pleased with myself. The blouse was the nicest thing I'd ever made.

'Your mam is going to get such a lovely surprise.'

The mention of Mam made me sad for a minute, but then I thought of the surprise she'd get when I gave her the blouse – and maybe even the cream for her hands too.

I folded the blouse and put it on the shelf in our little press. Then I put out the light and got into bed. It took me a long time to get to sleep, and all night

long I dreamt about the show, and winning the first prize.

* * *

When I woke, Nellie was already up and dressed and pulling on her boots.

'I can't be late,' I said, jumping up. 'What if I'm too late for the show?'

Nellie laughed. 'The show starts at three, and you don't have to bring the blouse there until two.'

'What time is it now?'

'Delia has just called me this minute – so it can't be six o'clock yet. I think you've got plenty of time, so go back to sleep and enjoy your day off.'

Any servant who could be spared was getting the afternoon off, but Nellie, like all the others would have to work hard all morning. As she left, I turned over and tried to sleep – but how could I? The day of the Home Industries show was here at last!

* * *

Soon I got up and put on my very best clothes – the lovely blouse Mam made me for my last birthday, and a skirt I'd made myself with fabric from Lady Mary.

The morning passed very slowly. In the end, Cook, who was always kind to me, chased me out of the kitchen.

'I know you're excited, love,' she said. 'But I've got to make two hundred jam buns, and I can't do that if you're under my feet talking endlessly about your mam's blouse.'

'Sorry, Cook,' I said.

'That's all right,' she said, as she handed me a slice of apple tart and pushed me through the door.

No one else had time to talk to me either, and I began to think I'd prefer to be at work.

I went for a long walk around the garden and down to the sea, and I wished my days off always passed so

slowly. When I couldn't wait any more, I fetched the blouse and made my way to the riding school, where the show was to be held.

The place was gone mad altogether. Men were carrying tables and chairs, women were laying out white cloths, and boys were running back and forth with jugs and vases and stacks of paper and pencils.

'You're early,' said a woman, when I found the table for hand-sewn garments. She didn't seem to mind though, so I held out my precious work.

'This is a woman's blouse for the competition.'

'Very nice.' I was disappointed she didn't even look at it properly, but decided she was busy.

'You can put it there, and fill in this slip of paper with your name – and whether the blouse is available for sale.'

For sale! I'd never thought that someone might actually pay money for a blouse I'd made. How much would they pay – and what could I buy with that money? For a tiny second I was tempted, but then

I pictured how Mam would love the blouse, and how beautiful she'd look wearing it. My lovely mam deserved the best thing I could ever make.

'It's not for sale,' I said. 'But thank you.'

I laid the blouse where she showed me and pinned on the label.

'Good luck, said the woman. 'Now off you go, and don't come back until three o'clock.'

* * *

I'm not sure anyone appreciated the mutton stew Cook had made for dinner. A whole Saturday afternoon off was a rare thing, and everyone was looking forward to it.

A few other servants had entered the competition. Johanna had knitted a pair of socks, which were going to be a surprise for Harry's birthday. Delia had made a plum cake, which looked delicious as it lay cooling next to the open window.

'Is something burning?' asked Isabelle, the children's maid.

'Oh Lord,' said Ita, running into the kitchen. 'That's my soda cake.'

She returned with a blackened lump on a tray, trailing dark smoke behind her.

'I wonder will it still be...?' Before Ita could finish the sentence, the cake rolled from the tray, landing on her foot, and making her squeal. It bounced once, then rolled to the corner of the room. I put my hand over my face, trying to hide my giggles, but kind Nellie jumped up, and put her arm around Ita. 'Never mind,' she soothed. 'Maybe baking isn't for you. I'm sure you've got lots of other talents.'

'Next year, I'll do a flower arrangement,' Ita said, smiling gratefully at Nellie. 'I think I'd be good at that.'

* * *

'Come on,' I said. 'We'll be late.'

'Don't panic,' said Johanna.

'We've got lots of time,' said Nellie.

They were both laughing, but they let me drag them along anyway. I felt so happy, as the three of us skipped in the sunshine, with our hair washed especially, and our best clothes on.

'Oh!' I said, as we got to the riding school. Words raced around my brain, but I couldn't say any more. It was so wonderful! There were crowds of people, all in their Sunday best, pushing and shoving and laughing. The balcony was decorated with garlands, and from somewhere came the sound of music and sweet, sweet singing. I could smell flowers and cut grass and cakes and soap. I quickly got separated from my friends, but it didn't matter. At that moment I didn't care if I ever saw them again, as I wandered among the exhibits, trying to keep my mouth closed with the wonder of it all.

I walked quickly past the boring tables with plates

of potatoes and turnips and marrows. I lingered a little at the flower arrangements and pot plants. I licked my lips when I saw the rows of cakes and bread. When I came to the table where my blouse was, I tried to look casual as I examined the other blouses in the competition. Some of them were so lovely, I began to doubt my own work, but then the crowd moved me on, and I didn't mind. I was having a marvellous time.

I thought of Mam, and my little brothers and sisters. How they would love to be here, with all the noise and excitement, and everyone laughing and happy!

Outside in the courtyard, I got myself a glass of apple juice and a jam bun, and sat in a corner, enjoying the sunshine and the bustling crowds.

'Lily, there you are!'

I looked up to see Maeve, with a smaller girl who was wearing a beautiful pale pink dress, with a matching hat.

'This is Stella,' said Maeve. 'Stella, this is my friend Lily.'

'Hello, Stella,' I said, standing up and brushing crumbs from my skirt.

'Hello, Lily,' said Stella, holding out her hand to shake. I took it, noticing that, like Maeve's, her skin was soft and smooth – the skin of someone who never had to work for a living.

'Do you live near here, Lily?' asked Stella.

'Well, my family lives a few miles away,' I said. 'But mostly I live here at Lissadell.'

'Are you one of Maeve's cousins?' she asked. 'She has so many, I can't keep track of you all.'

'No, I'm not Maeve's cousin,' I said, laughing at the wonderful thought. 'I'm a housemaid.'

Stella looked surprised, but tried not to show it. Her eyes opened wider, and her cheeks went pink. I knew she couldn't join up the thought of me being Maeve's friend, and a housemaid at the same time.

'Being a housemaid must be very interesting,'

she said.

'Not exactly,' I said. 'Mostly it's tiring and boring.'

I wanted to kick myself for saying such a stupid thing. Did I sound ungrateful for the good job I had? 'But the family is very kind to me,' I added.

After that, we stood there awkwardly. Maeve and I were usually relaxed with each other, but with this new girl standing between us, I didn't know what to do or say. I shuffled my boots, knowing they were dusty and worn. I tried not to think how wild my hair must look, after the running I'd done with Nellie and Johanna. I wondered if Stella could see that my skirt and blouse were homemade, while her clothes probably came from an expensive shop in Sligo or even Dublin. As the seconds ticked by, even Maeve, who was always confident, began to look uncomfortable.

'Stella has lessons with me at Ardeevin,' said Maeve.

She knew I knew this already. Maeve talked a lot

about Stella, and I'd often felt jealous of the friendship between them. Sometimes, when I was on my knees scrubbing and cleaning, I thought about the fun Maeve and Stella must have, reading books, learning about the world and playing tricks on Miss Clayton.

I wondered why Maeve had never told Stella about me. Was she ashamed of me?

'Oh,' I said suddenly, pointing across the courtyard. 'I'd better go. I see Nellie and Johanna over there. They must be looking for me.'

Maeve turned around. 'I can't see them,' she said. That wasn't surprising, as I hadn't seen them either.

'Bye,' I said. 'Nice meeting you, Stella. I hope you both have a lovely day.'

Then I ran off to find my friends, suddenly feeling light and free, which also made me feel a little bit guilty.

Chapter Seven

a bell was ringing loudly and everyone pushed their way back in to the riding school. I still hadn't found Nellie and Johanna, but guessed they couldn't be too far away.

The bell kept ringing until everyone was silent, except for a baby crying somewhere in the background. Lady Mary appeared on the balcony and began to speak.

All around me, people whispered things like 'Isn't she so lovely?' and 'What a fine lady she is!' and I felt proud because I saw her every day, and sometimes talked to her, and she even knew my name.

'As you all know,' she said. 'There are terrible things happening in Europe. Sir Josslyn and I weren't sure if we should go ahead with this show, but we did not like to disappoint the people who worked so hard. I

would like to think that those of you who are so good at knitting and crochet will use your skills to make gloves and scarves for our brave soldiers.'

Everyone clapped and cheered when she said this, but I was worried. This was only August; was the war going to last until winter came and the weather got cold?

Lady Mary talked about committees and work-teams, and thanked lots of people I'd never heard of. Finally, when I thought I was going to burst, she said. 'And now for the important part – the prizes.'

The prize-giving seemed to take forever. There were nearly fifty categories, and lots of them were quite boring. When a category was called out, it was easy to see who had entered, as men and women and young people held their breath, and stared at Lady Mary, willing her to say their name. I watched as winners went to claim their prizes, some heads down and shy and some stomping up the steps full of bravado. Lady Mary shook everyone's hand, and said

something nice about what they had done (which can't have been easy as some people won for producing heads of cauliflower and cabbage).

Delia appeared next to me just as Lady Mary announced the prizes for plum cake.

'I've got all my fingers and toes crossed for you,' I said.

'Thanks,' she whispered in a shaky voice.

When Delia didn't win any prize at all, I turned to hug her.

'It's all right,' she said. 'My daddy came home from working in England yesterday, and the cake is a surprise for him. He says my plum cake is the finest in Ireland – and that's what matters to me.'

Now Lady Mary was calling out the prize-winners for the knitted socks, and though I looked everywhere, I couldn't see Johanna, but when her name was called in second place, I heard Nellie shriek, and I could see her jumping up and down in the corner of the room. As Johanna went up to claim her prize,

Delia and I clapped like mad, and cheered until our throats hurt.

Mary-Kate's dress didn't win, but before I could find her to say sorry, I heard Lady Mary say the words that stopped me in my tracks.

'And now, the winners for the ladies' blouse.'

Around me, I could see that people were shuffling their feet and talking, but it was as if they weren't there. All I could see was Lady Mary's face.

'In third place...'

Even though I'd always wanted first place, now I'd have been very happy with third – but I didn't get it.

'...Mary Roche. Well done, Mary – that's a very fine piece of work indeed. In second place ... Sadie Rooney – you made a truly lovely blouse, Sadie, you should be proud of yourself.'

Mary and Sadie took their prizes, and came back down the steps, looking delighted with themselves.

Now I felt sick.

Was I going to faint?

I wondered if I should have offered the blouse for sale after all. If I didn't win, at least I might get enough money to buy cream for Mam's hands.

There was the sound of water rushing in my ears, and everything seemed to be happening in slow motion.

'First place in this section goes to...' Lady Mary checked the list in front of her, '... Lily Brennan!'

I looked around me in amazement.

Had I heard right?

Had I actually won?

Delia gave me a shove. 'It's you, Lily. You've won first prize. Go up there quick before she changes her mind.'

Moving slowly, as if in a trance, I pushed through the crowds towards the bottom of the stairs. Then I heard a familiar little voice. 'Lily!' And then another. 'Lily!'

Winnie? Anne? What were my sisters doing here?

This whole thing had to be a dream, and any minute

I was going to wake up in my little basement room, with Nellie sleeping soundly next to me.

But then, near the door, I saw Mam and my brothers, Denis and Jimmy. Mam had tears rolling down her face, and the boys began to chant and clap. 'Li-ly! Li-ly! Li-ly!'

Everyone began to laugh, but not in a bad way. My little sisters wriggled and pushed until they got to my side, looking so darling in the yellow dresses I'd made the year before. I went up the stairs with a little giggling girl holding each of my hands. Lady Mary laughed too. 'I think this is a popular win,' she said, as she handed me an envelope. 'Congratulations, Lily. You are a very talented young lady.'

And I thought I might faint away from happiness.

* * *

'What are you doing here?' I said when Mam finally stopped hugging me and telling me how great I was.

She smiled. 'One of the neighbours was coming this way on an errand, and he had room on the cart for the four of us, so here we are.'

'We can stay for two whole hours,' said Denis.

'Can I see the motor car?' said Jimmy.

'Are there any kittens?' said Anne.

Winnie didn't say anything at all, as she clung to my skirt and sucked her thumb.

Now Nellie and Johanna rushed over to hug and congratulate me.

'And well done to you too, Johanna,' I said.

'I think Johanna's socks were the best,' said Nellie loyally. 'She should have got first prize.'

Johanna smiled, and at first I thought it was because of what Nellie had said, but then I realised that this was a different smile – one she saved for someone else.

'Hello, Harry,' I said without turning around.

'How did you know I was…?' he began as he came up beside me, but Nellie and I only laughed.

I introduced my family to my friends, and we planned what to do for the next few precious hours. Johanna, Harry and Nellie took the boys to see the horses and the motor car, while the rest of us wandered around the riding school, as Mam wanted to see all the things people had made.

'Beautiful. Gorgeous. So lovely,' she said, as she admired all the entries, especially the ones with special labels, saying that they had won. When we got to my blouse, Mam was so quiet, I began to worry that she wasn't well. She touched the soft fabric, and ran her fingers over the frilled neck.

'It's a work of art,' she whispered. 'You're such a clever girl, Lily. Lady Mary is going to look so fine when she wears it, and I'm sure all her rich friends will think it came from the finest fashion shop in London.'

'But, Mam...,' I began, before stopping myself. I was looking forward to the surprise, and decided to delay it for another while.

'What, Lily?' she asked.

'Let's get buns and juice for you and the girls,' I said.

Winnie and Anne *loved* that idea, but Mam hesitated.

'Ah, girls, ye must still be full up after the bread ye had on the way here,' she said. 'And we'll have something else to eat when we get home.'

And then I understood. 'It's all right, Mam,' I whispered. 'It's free. Today we don't have to pay for anything at all.'

So the girls got their juice and buns, and the four of us sat in the sunshine, and everything was perfect.

'Oh, look, there's Lady Mary,' I said after a while.

'Is she...coming over here?' said Mam nervously.

'I think so.'

Mam jumped up, and spat in her handkerchief to wipe the girls' jammy faces, and they wailed and tried to pull away, just as they always did.

'There's a fine lady coming,' said Mam. 'So behave

yourselves for once.' Mam wasn't usually that cross with them, so I could tell how nervous she was.

'Lily,' said Lady Mary. 'This must be your lovely family. How nice to meet you all.'

Mam went red and put her head down, and mumbled something that none of us could understand. I love my mam more than anyone in the world, but right then I was embarrassed for her – and for me.

Lady Mary pretended not to notice, as she began to praise me, and say how good I was at my work. Then Mam couldn't stop herself.

'You're right, your ladyship,' she said with a huge smile on her face. 'Lily is the best girl in all of Sligo.'

'But what about me?' said Anne.

'And me?' said Winnie.

And we all laughed, and everything was fine.

* * *

I wanted that special afternoon to last for ever and

ever, but much too soon it was time for my family to leave. The boys were so excited about all they had seen, I knew they'd have Mam's ears worn off from talking about it all.

Anne was cross and tired, and little Winnie was asleep in Denis's arms.

'It's been so lovely, seeing where you work, and meeting your friends,' said Mam. 'I'll rest easy in my bed at night, knowing you're in such a nice place.'

'Don't go for a minute,' I said. 'There's one more thing...'

'But ...' said Mam.

'Won't be long,' I called as I ran off.

'What's this?' asked Mam, when I came back with a parcel wrapped in crisp new brown paper.

'Is it a cake?' asked Jimmy.

'Or a kitten?' asked Anne.

I gave Mam the parcel, and she opened it, carefully saving the brown paper so she could use it again. She held up the blouse, and it looked wonderful with her eyes and the bright blue of the sky.

'Your blouse,' she said, with a puzzled look on her face. 'I don't understand.'

'It's for you,' I said.

'But what about Lady Mary?'

'Lady Mary has hundreds of blouses, but that doesn't even matter. I made this one for you, Mam, only for you.'

Now tears came to her eyes. 'Oh, Lily, thank you,' she whispered. 'But it's so fine, and I don't know if I...'

'Mam, don't you see? To me you're the finest lady in the whole country, and you deserve this blouse. I want you to hold your head up and wear it often. Please.'

Mam hugged me. 'Then that's what I'll do. Thank you, my pet. Thank you so much.'

She folded the blouse again, and put it carefully in her basket.

'It's time for us to go,' she said. 'Goodbye, my girl.

Come along, children.'

They began to walk along the path, with brave Denis staggering under the weight of Winnie.

'Goodbye,' I called as I waved. 'I'll see you all next week.'

I watched until they were gone from sight, and then I turned to go back to Lissadell House, and my other life.

Chapter Eight

*N*ext morning, Maeve came in while I was tidying the drawing room.

'Stella liked you,' she said.

'I liked her too.'

'I'm going back to Ardeevin tonight, but when I get back, maybe one day Stella could come over here, and I could ask Mrs Bailey if you could come out with us. The three of us could walk by the sea, or Albert could take us for lunch somewhere.'

I smiled. It was kind of her to suggest it, but I knew it would never happen. Me being friends with Maeve was just about acceptable – and I knew this was only because Maeve was lonely, and because her mother spent her whole life breaking rules. Spending time with other friends of hers, though – I knew that would never work.

'I'm glad you won the prize,' she said then. 'You deserved it.' I knew the show and the prize meant nothing to Maeve, but she was being kind.

'Thank you,' I said. 'Mam came here, you know – to the show.'

'Oh,' said Maeve. 'I didn't meet her.'

I smiled. That wasn't an accident. Mam had enough to worry about, and seeing me with Maeve would have given her one more thing to add to the list.

'Is *your* mother planning to visit soon?' I asked.

'I don't think so. She and Uncle Joss are fighting again.'

'What's happened?'

'Oh, she thinks Ireland should remain neutral, and not get involved in the war. Uncle Joss believes the opposite.'

'Brothers and sisters don't have to agree on everything, I suppose.'

She gave a big sigh. 'That's true, but Mother has been making speeches, and setting up a new organi-

sation about neutrality for Ireland. Her opinions are printed in all the newspapers, and Uncle Joss really hates that.'

I thought I could see the beginnings of tears in her eyes. Sir Josslyn wasn't the only one – poor Maeve also hated her mother's fame.

* * *

'Have you been reading about Countess Markievicz?' I asked Harry later.

'It's hard not to,' he said. 'She's been in the papers a lot lately.'

'And what do *you* think about the war? Do you agree with the Countess or with Sir Josslyn?'

'There aren't any easy answers,' he said, putting down his iron and looking at me. 'War is bad, but there are terrible things happening in Belgium, and we can't stand by and watch.'

'Maybe the Countess is right, though – maybe

none of this is our business?'

'That's not the way I see it. If we let this happen, who knows what country will be next? If Ireland was invaded, who would come and help us? Sometimes you have to be brave, and stand up and do the right thing.'

'But you're doing a good thing here. You're working hard, taking care of the house and the Gore-Booths.'

He gave a strange laugh. 'My brother is working in England and he's going to join up. Soon he'll be fighting for a cause, and what am I doing? I'm carrying trays and folding shirts and ironing newspapers.'

'So you think you might...?

'Who knows?' he said, guessing what I was afraid to say. 'I need to have a long, hard think.'

* * *

The next week was very strange. Mr Kilgallon didn't allow talk of war at the dining table, but that didn't

make much difference. Servants whispered about it when he wasn't around, and Harry shared what he read in the newspapers and kept everyone up to date with what was happening.

Sometimes though, as I went to pick flowers for the house, or walked to the beach with Maeve, it was hard to imagine a world where men were killing each other. At Lissadell, all you could hear were the birds, and the waves, and the chatter of the little Gore-Booths as they played outside with Isabelle. At Lissadell, life went on as before.

* * *

But then, slowly, things began to change. Sir Josslyn went to a meeting in Ballymote and gave a big speech, encouraging young men to sign up and fight. After that, Mr Kilgallon couldn't stop us from talking about the war at dinner, and sometimes it seemed as if we talked of nothing else.

Then one day, I woke to a huge commotion.

'Oh, no,' said Nellie. 'I hope someone hasn't died.'

As soon as we had our uniforms on, we went out to the passageway, where we saw Mrs Bailey running around carrying long paper lists – which was never a good sign. From the kitchen we could hear Cook wailing. 'It's too many – and not enough notice!'

'What's happening?' I asked Delia, who pushed past, looking almost as anxious as Mrs Bailey did.

'The Connaught Rangers are having a big recruitment meeting in town, with a band and everything.'

'Sounds exciting,' I said. 'But what's that got to do with us?'

'They are all coming here for lunch!' said Delia.

Now I understood what the fuss was about. A nice social gathering for the Gore-Booths meant a whole lot of work for us servants.

* * *

Much later, Nellie and I were giving the hallway a final sweep when we heard the first of the motor cars.

'We should go back downstairs,' she said. 'Before they see us.'

I laughed as I pulled her behind a pillar. 'I don't care if they see us, but I *definitely* want to see them.'

We watched as Mr Kilgallon opened the front door and welcomed a huge crowd of men. Oh, how strong and handsome they looked with their fine uniforms and shiny boots! They were laughing as they talked about the crowds who'd lined the streets waving flags and cheering. Nellie and I stared in silence – it was like looking at royalty.

Sir Josslyn appeared and led the soldiers into the drawing room, closing the door firmly behind them – and Nellie and I went back downstairs to our work.

A while later I was called up to the drawing room to clean up some tea that had been spilled. The room was buzzing with the men's loud voices and the clatter of cups and plates, and nobody paid any attention

to me as I did my work. Then I saw Harry standing by the window talking to an older man with lots of stripes on the shoulders of his uniform. I was wondering what they were talking about, when I saw the older man take a leaflet from his pocket. On it was a picture of a soldier, and the words – *Remember Belgium – Enlist today*. Harry took the leaflet, and stared at it with a strange look on his face. Then Sir Josslyn called him, and Harry put the leaflet in his pocket, bowed to the older man, and hurried to clear the side table.

* * *

Late that night, as Nellie and I were in bed reading, Johanna came to our room.

'Johanna, what's wrong?' said Nellie. 'Have you been crying?'

I was on a very exciting part of my book, so I hadn't looked up as Johanna slipped into bed next to her

sister. Now though, I turned to see that Johanna's face was puffy, and her eyes were red.

'I think I got soap in my eyes,' she said. 'So careless of me.'

Nellie looked at me. We both knew that Johanna was lying, but what could we do? Johanna never liked to talk about herself, or how she was feeling.

'Harry is looking very smart with his new haircut,' I said. I was trying to make Johanna feel better, but instead, she put her hands over her face and began to sob.

'Johanna!' said Nellie. 'Is it Harry – did you two have a fight?'

Johanna was crying so much she couldn't answer. Nellie patted her back, and I saw that she too had tears in her eyes. Sweet Nellie had no idea what was wrong, but she hated to see her sister in pain.

I got out of bed and went over to my friends. I held Johanna's hand, and waited – though by now I was fairly sure why she was so upset.

'Whatever is wrong,' I said when she was a little quieter. 'You can talk to us.'

And then, through her sobs, Johanna told us what I had already guessed.

'Harry is joining the army and going to fight,' she said. 'Oh, girls, I can't lose someone else. I can't!'

Now tears came to my eyes too. Poor Johanna's life had been so hard. She'd lost her mam and her dad and her little sister, and she'd spent years in a workhouse, thinking that Nellie was dead too. What would she do if Harry ..?

'Johanna, I'm so sorry,' I said. 'Maybe he'll change his mind.'

She shook her head. 'He won't. He's such a fine and decent man. He believes he's doing the right thing, and nothing will put him off. I'm proud – but I will miss him so much.'

'When...?' began Nellie, but stopped because she was sobbing so much.

'He's already spoken to Sir Josslyn, and he leaves

first thing in the morning.'

I wished Harry could stay for a few more days, to give Johanna time to get used to the idea, but maybe that would never work – maybe she'd only be miserable for longer.

'Is he going to join the Connaught Rangers?' I asked. 'They looked so fine in their uniforms – and he wouldn't be too far away while he's doing his training.'

'No. Tomorrow he leaves for London, so he can sign up with his brother, Eugene. He says that way they can keep an eye on each other, keep each other safe.'

'That's nice,' I said, not sure if it really was. Can you mind someone on a battlefield? Can you tell the enemy not to shoot someone because you love them?

She started to cry again. 'When he told me he was leaving I had to give him the socks I knitted – even though his birthday is weeks away – he didn't open the package – he said he didn't want to spoil the sur-

prise – and now – now I won't see his face when he opens it – he'll be so far away, and...'

'Mr Kilgallon says the war will be over by Christmas,' I said, trying to sound like Mam cheering my sisters after a fall or a fight. 'Think of that Johanna – by the time Cook is preparing the geese for Christmas dinner, Harry will probably be back here with us – and a hero too.'

She hugged me but didn't answer. I couldn't think of anything else to say, but the same thought kept running through my head – what if Mr Kilgallon was wrong?

* * *

In the morning, Sir Josslyn and Lady Mary came downstairs to say goodbye to Harry, who was finishing breakfast with Nellie and me.

'You will be greatly missed, Harry,' said Lady Mary.

'But you are doing a fine thing,' said Sir Josslyn.

'Thank you,' said Harry, looking embarrassed.

'Have you everything packed?' asked Lady Mary.

'I have packed what I need for England,' said Harry, pointing to his bag which was all ready at the door. 'And I will go right now and pack up the last of my things to bring to my parents' house.'

'No need to do that,' said Sir Josslyn. 'This has been your home and there is plenty of space here. When we get a new footman he can have one of the other rooms, so yours will be ready for you on your return. Don't forget, Harry – go and do your duty and make us proud, and when you get back, your job and your room will be waiting for you as before. Now off you go, so you'll be in plenty of time for the train.'

'I'll be off then,' said Harry, when Lady Mary and Sir Josslyn had gone back upstairs. 'Goodbye, girls. I'll see you soon.'

I was close to tears and Nellie was already crying. 'Goodbye, Harry,' she sobbed. 'We'll all miss you so much.'

'Write to us – and come back safely,' I said. 'As soon as you can.'

'I'll be back when the job is done,' he said.

Johanna came in, looking pale and sad and afraid.

We all stood in silence.

I looked at Nellie.

Should we stay or go?

Did Johanna want us to be with her?

But how could we watch them say goodbye?

In the end, Harry decided for us.

'Johanna, will you do me the honour of walking me as far as the gate?'

She nodded, and he held the door for her and followed her out.

As he pulled the door closed, I wondered if I'd ever see him again.

Chapter Nine

The next few days were terrible. Johanna did her work, and answered when Nellie and I spoke to her, but it was almost as if she were a shadow of herself – as if the real Johanna was somewhere else, somewhere far away where we couldn't reach her. At night she slept in Nellie's bed, though in truth I doubt if she slept much at all, as I often woke to hear her sobbing.

And then one day she got up and put on her uniform in the old bright and brisk way we were used to.

'Thank you for letting me sleep here with you two,' she said. 'But tonight I will go back to my own room. Harry is being brave, and I must be brave too.'

Then she hugged us both, and went to bring Lady Mary her morning cup of tea.

* * *

More and more young men decided to join the army. A stable boy and an estate manager signed up with the Connaught Rangers. Every time I went home, Mam had another story about someone I used to know, who was now away at army training. I thought of Harry and all these brave men, and prayed that they would come safely back to us.

And yet, while the world was changing, for me the days passed slowly, with sweeping and dusting and tidying, hour after hour.

'Don't you get fed up of all this?' I asked Nellie one day as we mopped the front hallway.

'All what?'

'All this work! We mopped here this morning, and it got dirty, and now we're mopping again, and in half an hour's time it will be dirty again, and so on and on and on and on.'

'I don't mind mopping,' she said. 'I like seeing the

tiles all shiny and clean like new.'

'And if you're still here mopping in twenty years' time?'

'I wouldn't mind that either,' she said. 'In fact I think I'd quite like it.'

I sighed. 'I know we're lucky to have these jobs, but...'

'You still want to be a teacher, don't you?'

I nodded. 'I've wanted that since I was little, and I don't know if it will ever change.'

'Don't let it change!' she said fiercely, making me stop mopping and stare at her. 'Please don't give up on your dream, Lily. I'll miss you if you ever leave here, but I want your dream to come true, I really do.'

'Thanks, Nell,' I said, and then two of Sir Josslyn's dogs came skittering across the hall, leaving muddy footprints behind them, and I couldn't make up my mind if I wanted to scream or laugh or cry.

* * *

Then one day a letter came for Johanna, and she was so excited I thought she was going to faint away.

'You and Nellie can read it,' she said, when she came to our room that night, waving the envelope in the air.

'Are you sure?' I asked. 'Isn't it private?'

I'd never got a love letter in my life, but if I did, would I want to share it with anyone else?

Johanna smiled, and patted the pocket of her apron. 'Harry put in a special note just for me, and that one *is* private, but this one is for the three of us. He didn't want you and Nellie to feel left out.'

Nellie beamed, and I was happy too. I wanted to hear Harry's news, but more than that, I was glad that Johanna had fallen in love with such a kind man.

Johanna held the letter out to Nellie, but she shook her head shyly.

'You read it Lily,' she said. 'I want to concentrate on what he says, and not worry about making a mistake.'

So I took the letter and began to read aloud.

Dear Johanna, Nellie and Lily,

Oh how far away Lissadell seems these days. I'm in England, somewhere in the countryside, but I'm not allowed to say exactly where. (They read our letters before they are sent, and cut out bits that are supposed to be secret. Mam wrote and said that Eugene's last letter looked like lace when she got it!)

I sleep in a barracks at night. It's not very comfortable, as we only have a blanket between us and the floorboards and for the first few nights I barely slept a wink. I shouldn't complain though, as some of the men have to sleep in tents and it gets very muddy when it rains.

We are busy all of the time from when the bugle wakes us at 5.30. First we have to tidy up our quarters – I'm used to that from Lissadell, but some of the lads (especially Eugene) are always in trouble for leaving a mess.

We haven't got any uniforms yet, so we are wearing our own clothes. We have to keep ourselves tidy and smart, but again I'm used to that. Who would have guessed that being a footman would be such good training for the army?

Then we do lots of marching – I am so fit I hardly know myself – I think I could run to the top of Benbulben without breaking a sweat.

One day we had to march in public, and were told that only men whose clothes were in good nick could go. Eugene was lazy so he ripped a big hole in his only trousers, and he spent the afternoon in bed!

The best thing is being with Eugene – he is very funny and a good lad. Maybe when all this is over, the lot of us can go out on a jaunt – army pay is good, so I will be rich enough to buy tea and cakes for everyone.

I think that is all the news, and I have to go and shine my boots, though I can already see my face in them.

Goodbye (or cheerio as they say here)

Your good friend

Harry

PS keep reading the newspapers – when I get back I expect you all to be up to date with world affairs.

—

'That's the best letter I ever heard,' sighed Nellie

when I finished reading. 'And I'm already looking forward to the tea and cakes. I'll wear my best dress especially for the occasion.'

Chapter Ten

'**I**'m back! Did you miss me?'

'You're one of my best friends, Maeve,' I said. 'Of course I missed you.'

'Thank you,' she said, looking very pleased. 'And good news – I have a plan!'

One of the things I liked most about Maeve was the fact that she *always* had a plan – and it very often included me.

'Uncle Joss bought a new pony yesterday, and I thought you and I could go for a ride together.'

'Seriously,' I said, laughing. 'What's your plan?'

'I'm not joking. I know you might not have much experience of riding, but...'

'I've *no* experience of riding. There's a big black horse in a field near home, but he's a crazy animal, and all the kids are afraid of him. I've travelled in

our neighbour's pony and cart a few times, but apart from that...'

'You'll be fine, I promise. The pony is small, and Uncle Joss says she's very quiet – my cousins will ride her when they're big enough, but for now she's going to be mine – and Mrs Bailey says you can stay away for two hours, and...'

'So what are we waiting for?' I said, as I put down my duster. I wasn't sure I liked the idea of riding, but it *had* to be better than an afternoon of cleaning fireplaces.

Maeve laughed. 'Come on then – let's go. I've already asked the groom to have the pony ready. She's called Star.'

As we ran towards the stables, I noticed that Maeve was wearing a gorgeous dress of pale blue silk.

'Can you ride dressed like that?' I asked.

'Of course not. I keep my riding clothes in a room off the stables – and I've got a spare set for you so you don't have to worry about anything happening

to your uniform.'

I decided not to worry, as I hurried along beside her. I still wasn't sure about the pony, but Maeve's enthusiasm was refreshing after all the sadness of Harry and the war. We were young, and we couldn't be sad all the time.

'Why do you have special riding clothes, if you didn't have a pony until yesterday?' I asked.

'I've been riding since I was tiny, but my pony died last year. Mother bought me the riding clothes the year before that – luckily she didn't know what size I was, so they still fit me!'

By now we were at the stable yard, where Teddy, one of the grooms, was standing holding a *huge* animal.

'I thought you said the pony was small,' I muttered, but Maeve didn't answer, as she ran towards the pony and began to stroke her neck and whisper to her and say how lovely she was.

'She's a beauty all right,' said the groom. 'Don't be

afraid, Lily, she's as gentle as a lamb.'

I'd seen lots of wild lambs in my life, so that didn't make me feel much better.

Maeve ran inside to get changed, while the groom showed me how to hold my hand out to Star. 'That's it,' he said. 'Nice and slowly, with your palm turned up.'

My whole hand was shaking, but Star didn't seem to mind. She bent her head and sniffed my palm, and the warmth of her breath was a bit frightening, but also nice. Her lips were huge and wet, and soon I wasn't afraid any more. I stroked her neck the way Maeve had done, and then her nose too.

'She likes you,' said Teddy. 'Just be careful not to get too close to her back legs – if she gets a fright she might kick you – and I wouldn't want to be sending you back to Mrs Bailey with the print of a horseshoe on your face.'

'Trust me, Teddy,' I said. 'I wouldn't want that either.'

'What do you think?' said Maeve, appearing next to us again.

My mouth hung open, but no words came out. Maeve was wearing a very smart jacket, shiny brown boots and – something that looked like very baggy... trousers!

'Don't look so shocked,' she said. 'Mother had this outfit sent from London. Gaga and Uncle Joss don't approve of course, but they are very old-fashioned.'

Maybe I was old-fashioned too, as when I went inside and picked up the outfit Maeve had left out for me, I had *no* idea how to put it on. It was like a puzzle without instructions, and I was glad no one could see me as I struggled with the strange and complicated folds of fabric.

Ten minutes later though, as Maeve trotted through the woods on Star, and I cycled beside her, I wondered why skirts had ever been invented. Cycling was so much easier without the worry of catching a long dress in the spokes of the bicycle. In trousers,

Maeve was able to sit astride Star the way men ride, not the silly side-saddle way I'd seen Lady Mary and her friends do.

'Mother says that one day all women will be able to wear trousers – no matter what they are doing,' said Maeve.

I didn't believe that would ever happen, but as I cycled along beside my friend, I couldn't bring myself to argue. At that moment, nothing mattered in the world except the crunch of my wheels on the gravel, the sun on my face and the wind in my hair.

* * *

After a while, Maeve pulled on the reins, and Star stopped trotting. Maeve jumped off and smiled at me.

'Your turn,' she said.

'But I don't think I...'

'Are you afraid?'

I *was* afraid, but I didn't like to admit it to this girl who was hardly afraid of anything at all.

'It's just that I've never...'

'There's a first time for everything. Now lean the bike up against that tree, and hold the reins. Let Star see that you're in charge.'

I did as she said, hoping Star wasn't smart enough to see that if she wanted to escape, this would be a very good time to do it.

'Now what?' I said a minute later, when Star was still standing quietly next to me.

'Now give the reins back to me and put your foot in the stirrup.'

I didn't know what a stirrup was, but could only see one likely place for my foot.

'Not that foot,' said Maeve, trying not to laugh. 'Unless you plan to ride backwards.'

'Let's save that for lesson two,' I said.

After a few false starts, I found myself sitting on Star's back – and it was terrifying! Star was shuffling

from foot to foot, and every time she moved I was sure I'd be flung to the ground. I felt so high up, I'd surely be killed if I landed on my head.

'I don't like this.' I was whispering, trying not to hurt Star's feelings. 'Can I get off now?'

'You can if you want,' said Maeve. 'We could...'

'No,' I said suddenly changing my mind. Who knew when I'd get a chance to ride a horse again? 'I'm very scared, but I know I can do this. Can we walk for a little bit – but slowly?'

So Maeve held the reins, and led Star along the path, and before long I wasn't scared any more. Maeve was very patient, showing me how to keep my back straight, and how to tell Star which way to go.

'Can we go faster?' I asked after a while. 'Can we trot like you did?'

'I'm not sure. If you fall off and get killed, I'll be in a lot of trouble with Mrs Bailey.'

'And I'll be in a lot of trouble with Mam – especially if she sees me wearing these trousers.'

But we trotted for a little while anyway, and it was wonderful, and I thought I'd cry when I realised it was time for me to go back to work.

* * *

'Thank you so much, Maeve,' I said when Star was safely in her stable, and we were back in our usual clothes, walking towards the house. 'My brothers will be so jealous when they hear about this. They'd both love the chance to ride a pony.'

'Maybe you could buy them one?'

I turned to look at her. Was she joking? If that was a joke, it was a very mean one.

She saw my face, and went red. 'Oh, I know you couldn't buy one right now – but if you worked very hard, and saved up your wages, maybe after a few months you could...'

'I work very hard already,' I said. 'But I can't save any money because Mam needs it to buy food and

clothes for my brothers and sisters. Don't you under-stand, Maeve? No one in my family will ever have enough money to buy a pony – ever! And even if we did – where would we keep it?'

'Didn't you say your mam has a field where she grows vegetables?'

Now I was angry. 'It's not a field – it's a teeny tiny garden, you could hardly keep a chicken in it, much less a huge big pony.'

'I'm sorry,' said Maeve. 'I was only trying to be nice.'

'That's all right,' I said – except it really wasn't all right. If Maeve and I were friends, why was she always hurting my feelings?

I knew she didn't mean it, but...

* * *

'Did you have a nice time with Maeve?' asked Nellie when we were tucked up in our beds that night.

'The riding was great fun,' I said. 'While I was on

the pony I managed to forget all about the war – but.
… sometimes … Maeve and I …'

I wasn't sure how to continue. Nellie would never
say it, but I suspected that, like Mam, she didn't
think it was right for people like Maeve and me to be
friends. But then she surprised me.

'You and Maeve are very good friends,' she said.
'You shouldn't let anything change that.'

So I told her what Maeve said about me buying a
pony for my brothers, and again Nellie surprised me
by giving a big laugh. 'That's so funny,' she said.

'But my feelings were hurt!'

'I'm sorry to hear that, but it's not Maeve's fault.'

'Well it definitely wasn't *my* fault.'

'Don't you see, Lily? It's no one's fault. Life isn't
always fair. You have a mam you see every week, and
Maeve doesn't. Maeve has lots of money, and you
don't. I haven't got a mam or any money, but I've got
the best big sister, and the best friend anyone could
ever hope to have. We all have to manage with what

we've got, and try to understand when people hurt our feelings without meaning it.'

'Thanks, Nellie,' I said, feeling a bit better.

As my friend turned over and settled down to sleep, I thought how calm and steady she was. All Nellie wanted in life was for things to stay the same. Maeve was so different – all fiery and enthusiastic about new things. I smiled to myself. Life would be very boring if everyone was exactly the same.

Chapter Eleven

*D*ear Johanna, Nellie and Lily,

Well, I'm still here – still training – getting fitter and stronger every day. When I get back you won't know me – I'll have the newspapers ironed in jig-time.

At last I have a uniform and very fine it is too. You would think me very smart if you could see me wearing it. The colour is what they call 'khaki' and if you don't know what that is, it's a bit like mud. They say it's so we won't be seen in battle so I suppose that's a good thing. I could easily get lost if I wore it in the mucky fields around home, and that's for sure.

Mostly we are busy all day, but sometimes we get an hour or two off. Pity there isn't anywhere to go, as we seem to be in the middle of nowhere. A few lads are going mad, but I'm used to a quiet life so I don't mind.

Some of the men say the food here is the best they ever

had – and that says a lot about them. I miss Cook and her lovely fresh bread and chicken pies. Just thinking about them makes my mouth water and then I dream of home and feel a bit sad.

We haven't got real guns yet, but we have wooden ones cut to the right shape. We learn how to hold them and run with them, and carry them while crawling along the ground. Sometimes I feel like a boy playing at war, the way I did many years ago at home in Sligo.

I hope ye are reading the newspapers. Already there are Belgian refugees in England, and I expect they will be going to Ireland before long. We have to look after these people who have done nothing wrong except get in the way of the enemy army.

I hope you are all well.

Goodbye for now

Your friend Harry.

* * *

A week after Johanna got this letter, the first refugees arrived in Dublin. Edward, the new footman, let me see the newspaper, and it was so exciting to read about these exotic people coming to our own island.

But shortly afterwards, things got *much* more exciting.

'Lily and Nellie,' said Mrs Bailey early one morning. 'Lady Mary wants to see you in the drawing room, so straighten your uniforms and off you go.'

'What do you think she wants?' asked Nellie in a worried voice as we hurried up the back stairs. 'Do you think we're in trouble?'

Lady Mary was the kindest woman in the world. She saved Nellie from the workhouse, and brought Johanna to Lissadell so the two sisters could be together. Even though Nellie worshipped Lady Mary, she couldn't stop being afraid of her.

'I haven't done anything wrong, have you?' I said.

She shook her head, as I knew she would. Dear Nellie never did anything wrong.

'Hello, girls,' said Lady Mary. 'I don't have much time, so I will get straight to the point. I am on a committee that has been set up to welcome Belgian refugees to Sligo Town – and I have just heard that the first family will be arriving this week – much earlier than we expected.'

This was very exciting, but I didn't know what it had to do with Nellie and me.

'A small house has been provided,' continued Lady Mary. 'And I have volunteered to help get it ready for the new arrivals. Mrs Bailey is sorting out the kitchenware, and I will select some clothing that my little ones don't need any more. I would like you two girls to sort out the bedding and towels. You will need to pack enough for a family of six. Do you have any questions before you start?'

I had lots of questions, including one big one. The linen cupboards at Lissadell were piled high with all kinds of things – thick white towels, so soft you could nearly disappear in them, fine blankets of real wool edged with satin, very fancy embroidered sheets of pure linen, and simple cotton sheets that had been mended over and over again. How generous did she want us to be?

'Yes, Lady Mary,' I said. 'Which...?'

She smiled at me. 'I think anything that is good enough for you girls and the other servants, would be welcomed by these poor refugees. Please make a bundle and leave it in my study as soon as possible, so I can check everything.'

'I understand,' I said. 'Come on, Nellie.'

'Oh, and there's another thing,' said Lady Mary. 'Albert will be delivering the supplies to Sligo this afternoon. Tomorrow he will take me there, to make sure the house is perfect. I will need to bring some-one with me to make up the beds and do other jobs like this. Which one of you would like to come?'

I wanted to jump up and down and shout and beg to be allowed to go.

Imagine a day away from my usual work?

Imagine a journey in the motor car?

As far as Sligo Town?

Imagine seeing real live refugees all the way from Belgium?

Imagine talking to one (even if we couldn't understand each other.)

Imagine...

But then I thought of the many good times I'd had with Maeve. I thought how lucky I was to be allowed to teach in the sewing school. Nellie's days were all the same, so this was her turn. I felt like crying at what I was going to miss, but Nellie was my friend, and I knew what I had to do.

'You can decide between the two of you,' said Lady Mary, before I could say anything. 'Whoever is coming should be in the *porte cochère* at nine o'clock tomorrow. It will be a long day.'

* * *

Nellie stopped at the top of the servants' stairs.

'You can go with Lady Mary tomorrow, Lily,' she said. 'I know you want to.'

'I *do* want to,' I said. 'But more than that, I want you to go. You will have such a wonderful time.'

'I don't want to go,' said Nellie in a shaky voice.

'But...'

'You saw me in there with Lady Mary. I was too afraid to say a single word. What would I do if I had to be with her for the whole day? I know you're trying to be kind, Lily, and I thank you for that, but you would love the trip, and I would hate it, so...'

'But Nellie...'

Now tears came to her eyes. 'Please go, Lily. Please, please say you'll go.'

'Are you sure?'

'I'm certain sure – you go with Lady Mary, and when you get back you can tell Johanna and me all about it.'

Suddenly I felt sorry for my friend. 'I know you're

shy sometimes,' I said. 'But maybe, if you try very hard to be brave, after a while you'll be different. The more you practise...'

'Thank you, Lily,' she said, smiling. 'The thing is ... I love you ... but I don't need to be like you. I don't want to be different. I'm happy as I am.'

'I love you too,' I said, giving her a big hug.

Chapter Twelve

*L*ady Mary and I sat in the back of the motor car. Edward handed us each a soft rug for our knees, then he closed the doors, and went back inside.

'All set, Lady Mary?' said Albert, and when she said we were, he started the engine and we set off on our adventure.

Albert was whistling happily, and I could guess why. His mam lived in Sligo Town, and I knew he was hoping to slip away to visit her for a little while.

'How is it going at the sewing school, Lily?' asked Lady Mary as we drove out through the huge gates. 'Do you still like working there?'

'Yes, Lady Mary,' I said. 'I love it. The women are so nice, and their work is very good. I love teaching them, but one day I hope...'

I stopped talking, not wanting to seem ungrateful.

'You hope what?' she asked gently.

And then the words came rushing out. 'I always dreamed of being a schoolteacher – ever since I was a little girl. I love children, and dream of teaching them how to read and write and do sums, but...'

'What?'

'I don't think that will happen now.'

I was surprised to hear myself saying the words. Was I really admitting that my dream might never come true?

'Why wouldn't it happen? You seem like a very bright and determined young lady, and if you want something badly enough...'

'I had to leave school too soon. Mam needed the money ... and even if I'd stayed on for another few years, she could never afford to send me to teacher training college.'

'I'm sorry to hear that.'

I knew she meant it, and I felt bad. 'Oh, Lady Mary,' I said. 'You've always been so kind to me. I

know how lucky I am to have a good job – and working in the sewing school on Fridays is very special. I'm happy – I really am.'

She patted my hand. 'You're a good girl, Lily,' she said.

After that she stopped talking and began to write in a small notebook. Albert was singing by now, and I passed the time by looking out the window. I had walked and cycled these roads many times, but from the motor car, everything was so different. I felt like a queen in a chariot as we raced through the countryside, faster than the wind.

It seemed like no time before we came to roads I didn't recognise. They were busier, and lined with all kinds of houses and shops.

'Nearly there,' said Albert. 'Just down the end of this street.'

He stopped outside a small white cottage, not much bigger than Mam's. 'This is the one,' he said. 'Home sweet home for some lucky Belgian family.'

It was cold inside the house, and Albert set to lighting a fire.

'When that is done you may leave us, Albert,' said Lady Mary. 'Please give your mother my best regards, and tell her I hope the medicine I sent has helped her bad chest.'

Lady Mary and I explored the small house – which didn't take very long. Besides the kitchen, there were two bedrooms, one with a big bed, and another with three smaller ones.

'There are four children,' said Lady Mary. 'So two of them will have to share. Do you think they will mind?'

'They've just run for their lives, Lady Mary,' I said. 'I don't think sharing a bed will be a problem.'

She laughed. 'I suppose you are right. Now, where are the sheets?'

The boxes Albert had brought the day before were

stacked on one of the beds. Lady Mary searched through them until she found the sheets. She shook out the first one and began to lay it on a bed.

I was embarrassed. 'I can manage, Lady Mary,' I said.

She smiled. 'I'm quite sure you can,' she said. 'But it will be faster if we both work, won't it?'

She was right. Between the two of us, we had the beds made, the floors swept and the clothes and towels tidied away in no time.

'And now for the finishing touches,' said Lady Mary, as she went to the last box, and took out four toy animals, laying them on the beds in the children's room.

'That's kind of you, Lady Mary,' I said.

'I wish we could do more for these poor people,' she replied. 'Now come along, the train will be here soon.'

I followed her along the street to the railway station. When we got there, we saw that it had been

decorated with bunting and flags of red, yellow and black. Huge crowds of people lined the platform.

'Is there a celebration of some sort going on?' I asked.

'This is for the refugees,' she said. 'Everyone is trying to make them feel welcome.'

When people saw Lady Mary, they stepped back so we could get to the front of the crowd, and just as we settled into our spot, I heard the sound of a train approaching. Everyone began to clap and cheer and sing as the train pulled up to the platform. When it finally stopped moving, the crowd fell silent and for a moment, the only sound was the hissing of the engine. Everyone watched as a door opened and a woman and her children stepped down on to the platform.

'Welcome to Sligo,' shouted a man, and the woman shouted back at him. 'Yerra, thanks very much – but I've only been gone since the morning, visiting my sister in Collooney.'

Everyone laughed at this, and the man put his head down, embarrassed.

Now another door opened and a very worried-looking woman stepped down. She scanned the crowd, and looked relieved when she saw Lady Mary, who stood out from everyone else because of her fine clothes.

'Lady Gore-Booth?' she asked, and Lady Mary nodded.

'You must be Mrs Hill from the refugee committee.'

'That's me, My Lady.'

'This is a great day,' said Lady Mary. 'I have been practising my French all night long.'

'Fat lot of good that will do you,' said Mrs Hill. 'None of the refugees come from the part of Belgium where they speak French. It seems these ones speak Flemish, a language that doesn't sound like anything I've heard before.'

'So how do we communicate?'

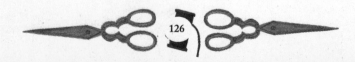

'Mostly by pointing,' said Mrs Hill.

Now more people stepped down from the carriage – a man, a woman holding a baby, and three small children. I couldn't help feeling disappointed. I'd expected these people to look exotic and different, but they didn't. They looked a bit like my own family, only thinner and poorer.

'Can you explain that they have to follow me?' asked Lady Mary.

'Sorry,' said Mrs Hill. 'I've got to get back on the train. There's another boatload arriving tonight. You're on your own.'

'Can you at least help them with their luggage before you go?'

'You're looking at their luggage,' said Mrs Hill, as she climbed back onto the train. 'I don't think they had much time to pack. Goodbye and good luck.'

The man and the two oldest children were each carrying a small bag, and that was it. As I stared at them, the oldest child began to cry, which set off the

others, and I learned that crying is the same in any language.

The poor mother looked close to tears too, and so tired that holding the baby seemed like an effort. The father looked lost and confused, and maybe a bit ashamed, as everyone stared at his family.

For the first time, I really understood why Harry had gone to join the army – to save people like this, poor people just like us, who were only trying to get on with their lives.

I stepped towards the woman and held out my arms. 'I love babies,' I said. 'Will I hold her for you?' I knew she couldn't understand me, but saying nothing would have been very strange. The woman gave me a weak smile and handed me the child, who looked surprised at first, but then stopped crying, put her dirty thumb in her mouth, and leaned against my cheek.

Now Lady Mary stepped forwards too. She took the woman by the arm, and gently led her towards

the exit, with me walking beside them. The man and the children followed, with no one speaking a word.

Oh, we must have looked a strange procession, as we made our way to the cottage, with a crowd of men, women and children following us, looking a bit awkward, and unsure whether they should be waving their flags and singing, or going home to their dinner.

Chapter Thirteen

When the family was safely inside the house, Lady Mary spoke to the crowd. 'These people will be very glad of your support over the next days and weeks,' she said. 'But for now, I think they need some peace and quiet.'

People seemed relieved to be told what to do, so no one argued, and they walked off, holding their flags by their sides.

Now a kind-looking woman appeared, carrying two large baskets.

'I'm Sadie, the priest's housekeeper,' she explained. 'I've brought food for our Belgian guests.'

Inside the house, Lady Mary took charge, persuading the parents to sit in the kitchen, with the children on the floor beside them, while Sadie began to prepare the food. The baby in my arms was asleep now,

so I lay her on one of the beds, carefully arranging the pillows so she wouldn't fall to the floor and split her head.

In the kitchen, the three other children looked so lost and afraid, I felt my heart would break at the sadness of it all. I thought of my own little brothers and sisters, and wondered would people be kind to them if they were driven from their home.

Then I had an idea. It didn't look as if anyone in the whole of Sligo spoke Flemish, so these children would have to learn English – and now was a good time to start.

I fetched the toy animals from the bedroom, and at the sight of these, the children perked up a little. They followed me to the corner of the kitchen where I sat them in a row on the narrow bench by the window. I sat on a stool and held up the first toy. 'Dog,' I said.

The children stared at me with huge dark eyes.

'Cat,' I said, holding up the second animal, but

again they didn't respond. I got down on my hands and knees, and crawled in front of them, miaowing softly. 'Cat,' I said pointing to myself. Then the youngest girl smiled and said a word in her own language. I tried to repeat it, and all three children laughed, and it was the most beautiful sound, which made the adults smile too.

I held the cat up again, and the oldest child, a boy, said 'cat.' I clapped my hands. 'That's it,' I said. 'You clever boy. It's a cat.'

I held the cat toward his little sisters, and they each repeated the word, delighted with themselves.

We played like that for a long time, and soon the clever children knew words for all the toys, and lots of other things in the room too.

Then Sadie came over. 'Sorry to interrupt the lesson,' she said. 'But the food is ready, and by the looks of these little ones, they could do with it.'

The Belgian family sat at the small table, and ate as if they hadn't had food for months.

The food smelled delicious, but when Sadie offered some, Lady Mary said 'no' for both of us. I wondered if this was because she wanted to spare the food, or if she didn't like to eat a meal prepared in a tiny cottage like this, which was half the size of the kitchen at Lissadell.

Lady Mary and I went to the door. It had been the most wonderful day. Did I dare to hope that we could come back again and again?

But then Sadie came over to us. 'Don't you worry about these people, Lady Mary,' she said. 'We were taken a bit by surprise, but now we know they are here, they'll be well looked after. There are good people in this town, and everyone will help to get them settled in.'

'I understand,' said Lady Mary. 'My driver will come here every Friday, and he'll bring food and anything else that is needed. Now come along, Lily. It's time we went home.'

* * *

Nellie woke when I slipped into our room and began to get ready for bed. 'Tell me every single detail,' she said.

'It was wonderful,' I said yawning. 'And do you mind if I tell you the rest tomorrow? I'm very...'

And then I fell into the deepest sleep of my life.

Chapter Fourteen

*D*ear Johanna, Nellie and Lily,

I hope you are keeping well. Thank you for your letters – they always buck me up when I am feeling homesick. It is getting cold so I am very glad of my lovely wool socks – I have to hide them from Eugene who has his eye on them too.

There was such excitement this week when our rifles arrived. Lee Enfields they are called. They are very fine, but part of me hopes the war will be over before I have to use mine in battle.

The officers are stone mad about us cleaning our rifles and give us special oil for it. They inspect them every day and pity any lad who has a dirty rifle! The officers are very cranky, but that might be because they are so old. Some had to come out of retirement to make up for the younger ones who have already gone to fight.

When the time came to fire the rifles, Eugene and I were the best, and hit all the targets first time. We've been shooting rabbits and pigeons since we were boys, but we kept that a secret between ourselves!

Well I must go now and clean my rifle.

Your friend

Harry

'I'm knitting more socks for Harry,' said Johanna, when I folded the letter and gave it back to her. 'I'm knitting every spare minute I get, so they'll be done quickly.'

'What about poor Eugene?' said kind Nellie. 'I'm sure his feet get cold too. Why don't you and I make him a sock each, Lily – that way we'll have a pair made in no time?'

I smiled at her. 'That's a good idea. Let's start tonight.'

* * *

'Might I have a word in my study, Lily?' asked Lady Mary when she found me sweeping the dining room.

As I followed her, I couldn't help feeling excited. Were we going to Sligo Town? How nice it would be to drive in the motor car, and see those dear Belgian children again.

'Thank you for your help yesterday, Lily,' she said, as she sat at her desk. 'I feel so sorry for those poor souls driven out of their homes. I'm glad to see that Sadie has stepped up – as long as she's in charge, our Belgian guests will be well taken care of.'

'Yes, Lady Mary,' I said. Of course I was glad the Belgians were being looked after, but disappointed that I wouldn't have any part in it.

'I was watching you while you played with those children yesterday.'

'I'm sorry if I forgot my place,' I said quickly. 'I know I'm a housemaid. I know you wanted me to clean and prepare the house for the family, but since it was all done ... and I felt so sorry for the poor little scraps.'

'No need to apologise, Lily. You have a special way with children. They learned all those new words, and you made it seem like a game. I was very impressed with what I saw.'

'Thank you, Lady Mary. If that's all, I'd better...'

'Michael is six now, you know,' she said. 'And Hugh is four. Sir Josslyn and I have been considering their education.'

I looked up at her, confused. Poor girls like me went to school until they left to go to work, but Maeve had a governess – as did all the rich girls I read about in books. Did Michael and Hugh need a governess too? Did Lady Mary think that I...?

And then the words popped out. 'Oh, Lady Mary. Thank you so much. I would *love* to be a governess. I would work so hard and I...'

She put her hand up and I stopped talking.

What was that strange look on her face?

Was Lady Mary embarrassed?

'Dear girl,' she said. 'I am so sorry if I gave you the impression that ... it simply wouldn't be...'

Now, as I realised my mistake, my cheeks burned as if they were on fire. Would Lady Mary tell Sir Josslyn what I had said? Would they laugh at me and tell their friends? Would I be mocked in all the big houses across Sligo?

'I was only joking,' I said. 'Of course I knew that...'

'Why don't you sit down?'

All I wanted was to get out of there as fast as possible, but I did as she said, perching on the very edge of a chair I had dusted a hundred times.

'I should have explained properly,' she said. 'What do you know about education for families like mine?'

'Not very much.'

'Then let me explain. The boys will have a tutor here at home until they are ten, when they will go away to school – most likely in England. In a few years' time, when the girls are old enough, they will have a governess who will stay with them until they

are eighteen or nineteen. Lily, you are clearly a very bright girl, but … oh how can I explain?'

'You don't have to,' I said, wishing the conversation could be over.

'You see – the tutor and the governess, they will be from families very different to yours. They will usually be from wealthy families who have fallen on hard times.'

Now I was even more confused. Were poor people who had once been wealthy better than poor people like me, who had always been poor?

'I know this does not sound fair,' she said. 'But these people will have been educated to a very high standard. For example, Sir Josslyn's sisters – Maeve's mother and aunts – had a governess who was a graduate of Cambridge University.'

I nodded. I'd never heard of Cambridge University, but I guessed I'd never be fetching up there.

'I'm sure the school you went to was very fine, but the governess needs to be able to teach subjects like

Latin and French and music.'

'I understand,' I said sadly. 'I spoke out of turn. If that is all?' Before she could answer, I stood up and began to edge towards the door. I wanted to be downstairs with Nellie and my other friends – with people like me.

'There *is* one thing. Michael should have a tutor already – but as he is an exceptionally sensitive boy, we have delayed this for another year. In the meantime, we don't want him to fall behind. Isabelle and the nurse can't help any more, as they have their hands full with Bridget, Brian and baby Rosaleen.'

I smiled. When I was younger, mam had five children to care for on her own, as well as cooking and cleaning for us all. Why did rich children need a whole team of people to care for them?

'Anyway,' said Lady Mary. 'I was wondering if you could spend a few hours a week teaching Michael and Hugh. Just simple things – some reading and writing and sums – so they will be ready for more

serious work when the tutor gets here.'

I stopped edging towards the door and smiled. Lady Mary was saying I couldn't call myself a tutor or a governess – but I couldn't care less. I could sit in the sweet little schoolroom upstairs, and teach those two darling little boys. For a few more hours a week, I wouldn't have to be a housemaid.

'Does that smile mean you are saying yes?' she asked.

'Oh, yes. Yes please. I would love that so much.'

'That is excellent. I have already spoken to Mrs Bailey, and she can spare you for an hour on Tuesday, Wednesday and Thursday mornings. On Fridays you will work in the sewing school as usual. You may start tomorrow at eleven o'clock. Now run along – I'm sure you have work to do downstairs.'

I was supposed to use the servants' stairs, but I was so happy, I skipped down the main ones, not caring if anyone saw me, not caring if I got into trouble. I was still a housemaid, but for a few hours every week, I

was going to be a real teacher too. A small part of my dream had just come true!

Chapter Fifteen

'**O**h, Mam, teaching those boys is such a lovely job.'

It was a few days later, and Mam and I were sitting by the fire, chatting while the potatoes boiled for dinner.

'Little Hugh knows some of his letters and numbers, and he is very quick to learn. Michael can read and write quite well already, so I'm teaching him geography. There's a globe in the schoolroom, just like the one the Master had, so Michael is learning all the countries of the world. The schoolroom is so lovely – with shelves and shelves all full of books.'

'I'm glad you're happy, child,' said Mam. 'But be careful.'

'Careful of what? Do you think one of the bookshelves will fall down and kill me?' Mam was always

warning me to be careful about something – even though I was all grown up and working for a living.

'Don't be cheeky, young lady! I don't want you to be hurt – that's all. You said the Gore-Booth boys will have a tutor next year – and that will be an end to your days in the Lissadell schoolroom. Oh Lily, I know you always dreamed of being a teacher and I am so sorry that wasn't possible, but people like us have to settle for what we have – that way we won't be disappointed.'

I didn't argue with Mam, but I didn't agree with her either. Life had already given me so many opportunities I never expected. When I first went to Lissadell as a housemaid, how could I have guessed that one day I would be working in the sewing school, or teaching the young Gore-Booth children? How could I have guessed that I'd have friends like Nellie and Johanna and Harry and Maeve de Markievicz?

I pulled my chair closer to Mam's and rested my head on her shoulder. She stroked my cheek and I

smiled. 'Oh, Mam, your hand is so soft.'

'That's from the cream you bought me. I wish you hadn't spent your winnings on me and the children, but I do love that cream.'

'Lady Mary says she'll pay me a little extra for teaching the boys,' I said. 'I can save it up and buy you more cream whenever you need it. So you see, Mam, things *do* get better.'

'They're always better when you're around. Now let's get moving, or it's potato soup we'll be having for dinner.'

* * *

As always, my day at home went too quickly.

'Let me help you button up your coat,' said Mam, as I got ready to leave. 'Or you'll freeze to death on that bicycle. Oh, and before you go, there's something I want to give you.'

I'd been hoping for this. My birthday was on Friday,

and of course I wouldn't be seeing Mam again until the day after that.

'Thanks, Mam,' I said, as she handed me something all wrapped up in brown paper. 'It's so soft. Is it...?'

'No clues! It's a surprise – so don't open it until Friday morning.'

'Friday is so far away. Can't you give me a small little hint?'

'Mam knitted it,' said Winnie, running in from the yard.

'And it's made of the nicest wool we ever saw,' said Anne. 'It came *all* the way from America.'

'That's enough out of you two scamps,' said Mam. 'Don't spoil the surprise for your big sister.'

But now I was very excited. 'How did you get wool all the way from America?'

'Peig Healy's daughter, Jane, sent it to her from Boston. No one's told Jane that her poor mother is half-blind these days, and can't knit any more. That's why Peig gave me the wool – though I don't know

why she picked me, of all the women in the village.'

'I know why,' I said. 'She picked you because you're always so kind to her.'

'Ah, get away with you,' said Mam. 'I like to be neighbourly. Now no more chat – if you don't get a move on it'll be the middle of the night before you get back to Lissadell.'

We went outside and I carefully placed the package in the basket of the bicycle. My brothers and sisters came out to say goodbye too. Winnie and Anne didn't cry when I left for Lissadell anymore, and that made me a little sad. Could they even remember a time when we all lived together?

* * *

Life passed more quickly now I had so many different jobs at Lissadell. Still though, it seemed like ages before the dark morning when Nellie woke me up with a big kiss.

'Happy birthday, Lily,' she said as she lit the gas light. 'Johanna and I put our money together and bought you this.'

She handed me a parcel which was clearly a book. This was a big treat, as I'd only ever owned a handful of books in my whole life.

'*Little Women*,' I read, after I'd carefully taken off the brown paper. 'I haven't heard of it before, but I'm sure I'll love it. Thank you so much, Nellie. You and I can start to read it together tonight.'

'There might be too many big words in it for me.'

'And I will help you with every single one!'

I jumped out of bed and went to the press where I'd put Mam's present. Nellie sat beside me as I began to unwrap it.

'Oh,' I said.

Inside the parcel was the most beautiful shawl I'd ever seen. As I moved it in the light, it was like the sea on a cold winter's day, changing from blue to green and back again. The tiny stitches were like lace,

and tears came to my eyes as I thought of my lovely mam, working by the oil lamp, late at night, when the children were fast asleep in their beds. I held the shawl to my cheek, and the wool was soft, like the fur of a puppy. Nellie took it from me, and gently wrapped it around my shoulders.

'Oh, Lily,' she sighed. 'You look like a fine lady. You look like...'

Just then there was a loud knock on the door.

'Nellie, where are you?' came Delia's voice. 'Mrs Bailey is looking for you, and she doesn't sound happy.'

Nellie jumped up and began to put on her uniform. As it was Friday, and I was working in the sewing school, I could stay in bed for another little while. I lay back and admired my book, and stroked my new shawl and felt like the luckiest girl in all of Ireland.

* * *

The wind was howling as I walked across the courtyard, but with my new shawl wrapped tightly around
my shoulders, I was toasty and warm.

'Hello, Lily,' said Maeve, as she came out another
door, and headed towards the stables. 'I'm back!'

'It's nice to see you. You've been away at Ardeevin
for ages and ages.'

'I know. Where are you off to?'

'I'm going to the sewing school.'

I'd been working in the sewing school on Fridays for months and months now, but Maeve never
seemed to remember this – which really annoyed me.
Then I felt my soft shawl, and couldn't be cross any
more. Maeve had lots of lovely clothes, but this was
as nice as anything she had in her many wardrobes
and drawers. For once in my life, I felt equal to her. I
pulled the shawl tighter, hoping Maeve would notice,
but she didn't.

'It's my birthday,' I said, stroking the soft shawl,
and turning slightly, so she could see how nicely it

fell over my shoulders and down my back.

'Happy birthday,' said Maeve, still not noticing. 'I hope you have a lovely day.'

'Mam gave me this shawl for my birthday,' I said. 'She made it herself – with wool that came all the way from America.'

Maeve didn't reply, and a strange look came over her face. She stared at me as if she hated my shawl – and me too.

'Don't you like it?' I asked, still not giving up.

'It's nice,' she said, wrinkling her nose a bit, as if she didn't mean a word of it. 'It was my birthday two weeks ago, and Gaga had a tea party for me at Ardeevin. I got *so* many presents. I got two new dresses, and some music books, a pretty brooch, my very own wristwatch and, oh, if I were to tell you all the presents I got, you'd be late for work. Anyway, I've got to go. Today I'm going riding with Uncle Josslyn. See you.'

As she walked away, I struggled to keep the tears

from my eyes. Maeve was supposed to be my friend, so why was she being so mean?

* * *

Mary-Kate was the only woman already at my table, and she looked up when I sat down beside her.

'Look at you, Lily,' she said. 'Have you been to a fashion house in Paris to buy that gorgeous shawl? You look like a real live princess and that's the truth.'

'Oh, Mary-Kate.' Before I could say another word, fat hot tears began to pour down my face. She put out her arms and wrapped them around me, and it was almost as comforting as being hugged by my own lovely mam.

'What is it, Lily?' she said, when she finally let me go.

'How can I tell you?' I said. 'I'm supposed to be your teacher – I can't be crying on your shoulder.'

'Ah, whisht! For the next few minutes, you're not

my teacher – you're my friend – and I want to know what has you so upset.'

So I told her the story, stopping every now and then to wipe my eyes.

'You must think me foolish,' I said as I finished. 'I know there's a war on, and I shouldn't be crying over something my friend said – or didn't say.'

'Now, now, don't be talking like that. In this life there are no rules saying what to be upset about. You're such a good girl, and I don't like to see you sad like this.'

'I don't understand. Why would Maeve be so mean to me? Why would she boast about all the fine things she has, on the one day I have something special?'

'Who knows?' said Mary-Kate, patting my arm. 'Sometimes friends hurt each other without really meaning to.'

Now Miss Connor came over, and I put my head down, hoping she wouldn't see my tear-stained face. She was a nice woman, but I was still a little bit

afraid of her.

'Lily,' she said. 'Is something the matter?'

'I...'

What could I say to her? I was supposed to be her assistant. What would she do if she thought I was a silly little girl crying over a fight with my friend?

'Everything is all right, Miss Connor,' said Mary-Kate. 'Lily was a little upset, but now she's fine again, aren't you, pet?'

I nodded, and Miss Connor looked doubtfully at my red eyes and puffy cheeks.

'If you're sure?' she said.

Mary-Kate's friendly smile made me strong for a moment.

'I'm sorry, Miss Connor,' I said. 'I'm ready to start work now. Mary-Kate, will you show me what you've done so far, and I then can teach you the stitches you need for the next part?'

Mary-Kate held out her work, and Miss Connor nodded and moved on to the next table.

'That's my brave girl,' said Mary-Kate, and her gentle words made me want to start crying all over again.

* * *

That night I told Nellie what had happened between Maeve and me. We talked about it for a long time, but, kind and gentle as Nellie was, she couldn't make it seem all right. Nothing she said could make me understand why Maeve had been so cruel to me.

Chapter Sixteen

'Please, Nellie, will you do Maeve's room this morning?'

Nellie and I were standing at the top of the servants' stairs with our mops and buckets and dusters, ready for an hour of cleaning bedrooms.

'Why are you whispering, Lily?' she asked. 'Everyone should be down at breakfast by now.'

'I know but ... anyway, will you do Maeve's room?'

'But you always do hers.'

'I know, but will you do it today – please – just in case she's still in there?'

Usually I loved when Maeve was in her room when I went in to clean. We'd chat together, and often she helped me to tidy up and make the bed. This morning was different though. This morning she was the last person in the world I wanted to see.

'But if you meet Maeve – maybe you could talk about what happened?' said Nellie. 'She's your friend, Lily, and you should make things all right between the two of you.'

'That's up to her, not me. *I* didn't do anything wrong.'

'All right,' sighed Nellie. 'I'll do Maeve's room this morning. Now come along, or we'll be up here all day.'

Just then, the door of Maeve's room opened. She looked beautiful, in yet another dress I'd never seen before. 'Oh,' she said when she saw us. 'Hello, Lily. Hello, Nellie.'

I waited for Maeve to say sorry for what had happened, but she didn't – she didn't say anything else at all. She stood there for a second, and then hurried along the corridor and down the main stairs.

'Are you all right, Lily?' asked Nellie gently.

Of course I wasn't. I was sad and angry and sorry for myself all at the same time. But in answer to Nel-

lie's question I just nodded, afraid that if I said anything I'd start to cry again.

* * *

The next few days were strange. I knew Maeve was
in the house, but I didn't see her. Lissadell was a big
place, and it was easy to disappear. Maeve never came
skipping down the servants' stairs, persuading Mrs
Bailey to let me join her in some mad excursion. She
never sneaked up behind me, covering my eyes and
asking me to 'guess who?' Sometimes I heard her
voice in the distance, and once I heard Lady Mary
calling her name, but I didn't see her, and we never
spoke.

And then one morning Nellie came out of Maeve's
room, looking puzzled. 'Maeve's bed wasn't slept in
last night,' she said. 'The place hasn't been touched
since I was here yesterday.'

Just then Isabelle came along, carrying baby

Rosaleen. 'I saw Maeve leaving in the motor car yesterday,' she said. 'She's gone back to Ardeevin. I heard her say to Lady Mary that she won't be back at Lissadell for ages.'

I wanted to ask Isabelle if she'd heard anything else. I wondered if she'd noticed whether Maeve looked sadder than usual, as if she might be upset by something, but then the baby began to cry – very loudly for such a tiny thing. 'Sorry,' said Isabelle. 'I have to go, or this one will bring the roof in on top of us.'

As she hurried away, Nellie took my hand. 'I'm sorry, Lily,' she said. 'I'm sorry Maeve didn't say goodbye to you.'

'That's all right,' I said. 'I'm fine. I've got you and Johanna, so I don't need Maeve in my life.' But this wasn't true. I was cross with Maeve – but I missed her very much.

* * *

As we finished dinner the next day, Edward brought in a letter and gave it to Johanna. She opened it and quickly read the two sheets. When she was finished, she folded one and slipped it into her pocket. The other one she handed to me without saying a word. I was excited to hear Harry's news, so didn't pay much attention to her silence.

'Let's go to my room and read it together, Nellie,' I said. 'Is that all right, Mrs Bailey?'

'Ten minutes – no longer,' said Mrs Bailey, but she was smiling, so I thought maybe we'd get away with a few extra minutes without any fuss.

'Thank you,' I said, jumping up. 'Do you want to come, Johanna?'

She nodded and followed us from the room. As we all sat on Nellie's bed, I looked at Johanna properly. Were those tears in her eyes? We all loved letters from Harry, so why was this one making her cry?

'Johanna?' said Nellie, noticing the tears too. 'Are you all right? Is it Harry? Did something...?'

'Read the letter,' said Johanna.

So, with shaking hands, I held out the letter and began to read.

Dear Johanna, Nellie and Lily,

This will be a short letter, as they have just told us we'll be shipping out in the morning, and everyone is rushing around like mad things. We have not been told where we are going, so even if I was allowed to tell you, I couldn't! In a way I am glad the waiting is over. I wasn't doing much to help the poor Belgians by sitting in this place polishing my gun over and over and digging trenches and filling them in again. Some of the lads are very excited and some are scared – and I'm not really sure how I feel – a bit of both, I suppose.

Eugene says hello to you all. I've let him read your letters, so he says you are his friends now too. I will write again as soon as I can – but I don't know when that will be.

Anyway, I'm still hoping that this will all be over

*soon, and I will be back with you girls, in the life I love
so much.*

Your friend

Harry

*PS Thank you for the socks you sent, and Eugene says
thanks for his too – they will keep us warm if it's cold in
the place we're going that I can't name.*

By the time I'd finished reading, tears were rolling
down Johanna's cheeks.

'I've been missing Harry so much,' she said. 'But
I didn't mind, as I knew he was safe. When he was
training, the worst that could happen was that he'd
be lonely, or bored ... and I was hoping that maybe
the war might be over before he was trained ... so he
could come back to us without ever fighting at all
and we could laugh about all that time he wasted.
But now ... if he goes to France or Belgium, or wherever ... oh, girls! I've seen the newspapers. I know
what it's like ... men are dying out there! If Harry ...'

I wanted to find words that would make Johanna feel better, but what could I say? There was a war on, and the man she loved was going to be part of it. I put my arms around her and held her close, while Nellie patted her back. It was all we could do.

Chapter Seventeen

*I*n the morning, Lady Mary came along the corridor just as I finished cleaning her bedroom.

She was carrying a large bundle of children's clothes and toys.

'Ah, Lily,' she said. 'I know you are supposed to be teaching Michael and Hugh this morning, but I'd prefer if you didn't.'

Teaching the two boys was the best part of my days, and hearing these words from Lady Mary made me want to cry. I wondered what I had done wrong, and if there was any way of fixing it.

'I'm sorry, Lady Mary,' I said. 'Are you not happy with my work? I know Master Hugh was tired and played up a bit yesterday, but little boys often do that, and he's...'

'I'm very happy with your work, and the boys love

you,' she said. 'But today I am going to Sligo Town to talk to Sadie and the refugee committee. It looks as if there will be more families arriving from Belgium soon, and I'd like to see what I can do to help.'

'Yes, Lady Mary,' I said, hardly daring to hope.

'My friends have all donated some things, and they are being stored in a house near the railway station. I thought perhaps you could come with me, and help to sort them out – would you like to do that?'

'Oh yes, Lady Mary! Just give me one minute to change out of my uniform, and to get my coat.'

'You can have five minutes,' she said, smiling.

And I gathered my cloths and dusters and hurried away, before she had time to change her mind.

* * *

In Sligo, the kitchen was small, but it was piled high with boxes and bags. Albert helped us to carry them into the bedroom, which had two beds in it.

'Thank you, Albert,' said Lady Mary. 'That will be all for now. Can you be ready to drive us back at three o'clock?'

'Yes, Lady Mary,' he said, and then he hurried off to visit his mother.

Lady Mary rolled up her sleeves, and opened the first box. 'Let's get started,' she said. 'Shall we put bed-linen and towels over there, and divide the clothes into men's, women's and children's?'

And so we set to work. After a minute it didn't seem strange to be working with Lady Mary, though I couldn't chat with her the way I would with Nellie. We folded everything neatly, and laid it in the correct pile.

'Look at this, Lily,' said Lady Mary after a while, holding up a gorgeous blue dress with pearly buttons on the collar. 'Don't you think it's pretty?'

I sighed. I thought *all* the clothes were pretty – and that dress would have been lovely on one of my little sisters. For a second I hoped Lady Mary could

read my mind, and would say I could have the dress, but then I felt bad. My family was poor, but at least we hadn't been run out of our country by men with guns. How could I take a single thread from the poor, homeless Belgians?

* * *

'Finally!' said Lady Mary, folding a crisp white shirt and placing it on the pile of men's clothes. 'This is the last one.' Then she looked at her wrist-watch. 'And just in time too. I have to get to my friend's house for a committee meeting.'

'Yes, Lady Mary,' I said, wondering what I should do. Was I supposed to sit here amongst all the clothes, and wait for Albert to get back?

Then my stomach made a very loud rumbling sound.

'Oh, you poor girl,' said Lady Mary. 'Sometimes I forget how hungry young people get. There's a hotel

on the next street, so perhaps you should go there and get yourself a bowl of soup, or a dish of stew.'

I stared at her.

Did she think I was brave enough to go into a hotel all on my own?

What would I say?

Where would I sit?

What would I use to pay for the food?

But then she reached into her purse and took out some coins. 'Here,' she said. 'This should be enough.'

'I can't take it, Lady Mary,' I said. 'It's too much, and...'

'Don't be silly. If you were at Lissadell, you'd be eating one of Cook's lovely dinners, so take this and buy yourself something nice to eat.'

I was going to protest again, but my stomach gave another loud grumble, and I knew I had to take the money, and find the courage to go into the hotel.

'And if there's anything left, please keep it and buy yourself something nice,' she said. 'Now off you go,

and I will see you here at three o'clock.'

* * *

I felt very fine and grown-up as I walked along the street, with the coins rattling in my pocket. I looked in the windows of the shops I passed, admiring all the pretty things, and pretending to be a rich lady, who could go in and buy anything she wanted – even if she didn't need it at all.

One shop had a display of ribbons – so beautiful it almost took my breath away. There was a green velvet one that would be so lovely in Nellie and Johanna's red hair, and a blue one that would be perfect for Maeve – but I pushed that last thought away – I didn't want to think about Maeve on my special day out.

I leaned in closer, and suddenly the shopkeeper waved and tapped on the glass. I jumped back, afraid. Was looking in the windows not allowed? Did she

think I was a thief? I realised I didn't really want to know, so I began to walk away quickly. Behind me I heard the tinkle of a bell as the door of the shop opened, and then I heard a voice.

'Lily! Come back here right now, Lily Brennan.'

I was tempted to run, but decided that would make me look even more guilty of some crime I didn't understand.

Then I stopped walking.

This was very strange.

How did the shopkeeper know my name?

I turned slowly, and was almost knocked to the ground as she ran up and threw her arms around me. 'Lily! Where are you off to and I only trying to call you?'

'Rose?' I said, pulling away so I could see her face.

She was smiling and her eyes were twinkling the way they had ever since we were tiny children together.

'Who else did you think it was? Why would a

stranger be running down the street after you?'

I told her what I thought and she laughed. 'Oh, Lily,' she said. 'I miss you. What are you doing here? Can you stay a while?'

'I can stay until three o'clock,' I said. 'But don't you have to mind the shop?'

'I haven't had my dinner break yet – let me go and ask my uncle if I can go now.'

She was back a second later, wearing her coat and carrying a pretty handbag. 'All set,' she said. 'What will we do?'

'If I don't eat soon, I might well starve to death.'

She laughed. 'We could go to my aunt's house, or...'

Usually I'd have loved a visit to her aunt's house, but now that Rose was with me, the hotel didn't seem so terrifying.

'Or we could go to the hotel?' she continued.

'Hotel!' I said.

'Then hotel it is,' said Rose, as she took my hand and we set off down the street.

Rose had been to the hotel before with her aunt and uncle, so she knew what to do, and what to say, and what food to ask for. Before long, we were sitting at a table in the corner of the dining room, and my tummy was quiet and satisfied after lots of bread and soup. I'd checked the prices, and knew I'd have enough of Lady Mary's money left to buy ribbons for my friends too.

I sat back in my seat and gave a big happy sigh. 'Look at us, Rose – all grown up and sophisticated.'

'I'm so happy to see you, Lily,' she said. 'If only Hanora were here, it would be perfect – just like it used to be when we were all together.'

For a while we talked about Hanora, and how she was getting on in New York, and how we loved the letters she wrote every month. Then we talked about our school days, and all the fun the three of us had together. I began to wish I could make the clock go

backwards – that my school days could be here again, days when life was easier, and everything seemed possible – but then I understood that could never happen. I remembered the little girl who'd felt foolish for going to the front door of Lissadell House, and for thinking that Albert, the driver, was the owner. I remembered the little girl who didn't know how to put on her housemaid's cap or apron, or how to clean a fire or make a bed when it's piled high with blankets and pillows. I couldn't be that little girl again – I was older, and different, and I could never go back.

Rose seemed to understand that too. 'Tell me what your life is like now,' she said. 'Is Lissadell different now there's a war on?'

'One of the footmen has gone to fight,' I said. 'He's our friend and we all worry about him, but otherwise things are much the same.'

'Do you still find the work boring?'

That reminded me. 'Oh, now I teach the little Gore-Booth boys. They have their own dear little school-

room, full of books and pencils and everything they need.'

'That's great news, Lily!' she said, clapping her hands. 'You're a teacher, just like you've always wanted.'

'It's true – I *am* a teacher, but only for a few hours a week. Next year, the boys will have a tutor, and when the girls are old enough they'll have a governess.'

'So what will happen to you?'

'I'll still teach at the sewing school on Fridays, but the rest of the time I'll be a housemaid. I'm used to that now, so it won't be too bad.'

'I know you like teaching at the sewing school,' she said. 'But what about teaching little children, in a school like the one we used to go to? Isn't that your dream anymore?'

'I'm older now. Being a housemaid isn't the worst life – and everyone at Lissadell is very nice.'

'I'm sure Lissadell is lovely, and many people dream of working there – but that's not *your* dream, Lily!'

'Dreams don't always come true,' I said sadly.

'Well your dream *definitely* won't come true if you give up on it.'

She sounded so fierce I had to laugh. 'I'm glad you care, but...'

'I sat next to you at school for eight years. When we met, you were a tiny little girl with the sweetest long plait all down your back. I knew you before you could read or write or anything. I knew you when you still had your baby teeth. You changed so much in all our time at school, but one thing *never* changed – your dream of being a teacher.'

'But...'

'Even the Master and Miss O'Brien could see it. They said you were born to be a teacher.'

'But Mam hasn't enough money for me to train as a teacher. How could I possibly?'

'Oh, I don't know, Lily. All I know is you can't give up. If you give up, you'll never be a teacher – and that would be a terrible thing.'

She was right – how had I let my dream fade away? I sat up straighter and smiled at her. 'I won't give up,' I said 'I'm *never* giving up. One day I'll be a teacher, and you can get married and move back home and have ten children and I'll teach them all, and I'll never be cross, even if they are as bold as you were when you were little, and they break my heart every single day!'

Chapter Eighteen

*D*ear Johanna, Nellie and Lily,

Sorry it has been so long since my last letter – you all seem so far away I'm not even sure what I should write, and how I could explain the way I live now.

I don't want to give out about this place, but I can say I'm sorry I complained about the barracks where we did our training.

It has been raining a lot and I am wet as I write to you so I hope the ink isn't all smudgy. They have given us good strong boots, but even so, some men have cold feet. There is also a terrible thing called trench foot – I won't describe it more for fear of upsetting ye. It comes from having cold and wet feet, and the only way to avoid it is to have plenty of spare dry socks to change into. Luckily Eugene and I are fine because of those fine wool socks you sent us.

Sometimes we go out to dig trenches and that is not a

nice job. I never minded digging to plant potatoes when I was home with Mam and Dad, but digging so men can fight is a very different thing.

We haven't seen any real action yet, but sometimes we hear the sound of shells in the distance – and I don't mean the kind of shells Johanna and I used to collect on Lissadell beach.

The food is not very good, but maybe I am spoiled after Cook feeding me for so long. We eat a lot of what they call biscuits – which are very hard and a bit like what the dogs at Lissadell get. One lad broke his teeth eating them, so now we soak them in our tea first. We also get a kind of soup called maconochie. It's not too bad if it's hot, but sometimes it's cold when we get it. It's not nice, but as my mam always said, 'hunger is the best sauce'.

When it's quiet we play cards, but sometimes I am bored – who thought you could be bored in the middle of a war?

My best comfort is being with Eugene. I am glad we are together and we will be able to look out for each other

the way we did when we were boys.

Well that's about it for now. I hope you are all keeping well and thank you for your letters – they make me sad and happy at the same time.

Your friend

Harry

I folded the letter and gave it back to Johanna.

'It doesn't sound *too* bad, I suppose,' I said.

She shook her head. 'That's just Harry,' she said.

'What do you mean?' asked Nellie.

'He won't want to worry us,' said Johanna. 'He's making it sound better than it is, just to make us feel better. He's such a kind man that even in the middle of a war, he's thinking about us.'

'He *is* a very kind man and I'm glad he hasn't got cold feet,' agreed Nellie, holding up her knitting. 'I'm nearly finished another one – I'm even getting good at turning the heel. Harry and Eugene will have the warmest feet in the whole army – and they will never

get that awful trench foot thing!'

'That's very sweet of you, Nellie – and you too Lily. I know they appreciate all the socks you have sent them.'

'I'm going to make vests for them next,' said Nellie. 'Fine warm vests, so if there's such a thing as trench chest, our boys won't have to be worried about it.'

'I wish we could do more,' I sighed. 'Sitting here knitting doesn't seem like enough.'

'I know,' sighed Johanna, who was also knitting as fast as she could. 'Why can't this war come to an end? Why can't people just get along with each other? Why can't Harry come home to us?'

She had tears in her eyes, and I wasn't sure how to make her feel better, so I held her hand – because sometimes that's all you can do

* * *

'Wake up girls. Get a move on.'

I'd been dreaming of a lovely summer day by the seaside with Mam and my brothers and sisters, so I wasn't happy when I woke up and realised I was at Lissadell, and it was December.

Delia pushed open the door. 'Come on, girls,' she said. 'Mrs Bailey is looking for ye – and she's got a big long list in her hand.'

Nellie and I jumped out of bed and began to dress. I barely noticed how dark it was and how cold the floor felt under my bare feet.

'At last!' said Mrs Bailey five minutes later when we reported to her. 'I've just heard that we're going to have even more visitors coming for Christmas, and there's a lot to do.'

'Is Countess Markievicz is coming?' I asked.

'I'm not sure it's any of your business, Lily,' said Mrs Bailey. 'But the Countess will not be joining us this year.'

For a minute I felt sorry for Maeve, but then I pushed that thought away. On Christmas Day I

wouldn't be seeing my mam either – I'd be at Lissadell, working hard as usual, and I wasn't sure if Maeve would know or care.

'Hurry along,' said Mrs Bailey. 'Today you have your usual work to do and you'll have to get started on all those extra rooms too. Now look smart, and gather your mops. Those rooms aren't going to clean themselves.'

* * *

The next few weeks passed very quickly. 'Time flies when you're having fun,' laughed Nellie every morning, when we were dusting yet another room, and cleaning another fireplace.

Maeve came back, but our paths rarely crossed. Often the only sign I saw was that her bed had been slept in, and there was a crumple of worn clothes on the floor in her dressing room.

'You should make up with Maeve,' said Nellie for

the twentieth time, as we swept and dusted the bed-room corridor. Doesn't your mam have a wise saying about things like this?'

'Mam has a wise saying about everything,' I said. 'She says you should never let a sun set on a disagree-ment – but so many suns have risen and set on this one, it doesn't matter anymore.'

'But you and Maeve were friends for such a long time.'

'More than a year,' I said sadly.

'And you always had such fun together. Remember when she taught you how to ride the bicycle? And when you went paddling and fell in the water? Every time you came back from an outing with Maeve, you were glowing – as if you'd been set free for a while.'

I smiled at the memories. 'That's exactly how it felt.'

'So talk to her. Make things right again.'

I shook my head. 'Our lives are too different.'

'That didn't matter before, and anyway, you and I

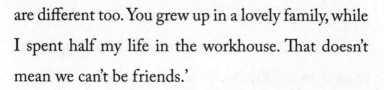

are different too. You grew up in a lovely family, while I spent half my life in the workhouse. That doesn't mean we can't be friends.'

'You and I will *always* be friends,' I said.

'So take the advice of a good friend,' she said, smiling.

'Even if I wanted to, it wouldn't matter. Maeve doesn't want to be friends with me.'

'How do you know?'

'If she wanted to be my friend she wouldn't have been so mean about the lovely shawl Mam made me. She wouldn't keep forgetting how poor I am compared to her, and how different my life is to hers.'

'But maybe...'

Before she could say any more, the door of Maeve's bedroom opened, and she came out. Nellie winked at me and hurried away, muttering something about cleaning the servants' staircase. I wanted to run after her, but stopped myself. I had nothing to be ashamed of.

As always, Maeve looked lovely, with her long hair brushed in shiny waves over her shoulders, and wearing yet another dress I'd never seen before. She was carrying a pretty purse, covered with beads that twinkled as they caught the light. I couldn't help glancing at my apron, which was stained from cleaning fireplaces. I couldn't help touching my cap, which was pinned tightly to my head, hiding most of my hair. I couldn't forget that instead of a gorgeous beaded purse, I was holding a sweeping brush and a duster.

'Hello, Lily,' said Maeve in a friendly voice. 'How are you today? There's ... there's ... something ... I'd like to say to you. It's important. I'd like to explain why I ... well ... maybe later on ... you and I could ... go for a walk together? I can ask Mrs Bailey if it's all right.'

Maeve looked shy and embarrassed, nothing like the confident girl I was used to. I knew she wanted to say sorry for her behaviour. Part of me wanted to hug her, and say how much I'd like to walk with her, and

how I'd missed her, and how many things I wanted to tell her – but the part of me that couldn't forget the hurt and anger was the part that replied.

'Thank you, Miss Maeve, but I'm very busy today.'

She looked at me as if I'd slapped her. I knew when I called her 'Miss Maeve' I had built a wall between us that might never again be broken down.

'Very well,' she said, looking hurt.

I watched as she walked away, and when she was out of sight, I slammed my sweeping brush against the floor in a temper.

'Lily?' said Lady Mary, appearing at exactly the wrong time. 'Is everything all right?'

'Sorry, Lady Mary,' I said. 'I dropped my brush. It won't happen again.'

She smiled at me and walked away, leaving me to get on with my job.

Chapter Nineteen

*D*ear Johanna, Nellie and Lily,

Thank you for all the new socks and the vests. Eugene and I might not be the best soldiers here, but we are definitely the warmest.

Please thank Cook for the lovely cake she sent – Eugene said it was the nicest cake he ever had, but if you ever meet our mam you can't tell her that!

I am spending much of my time in the trenches these days. It's very strange, living half under the ground like some rabbit who is not very good at burrowing. Not far away are the enemy trenches – so close we can sometimes hear them talking in their own language. (You learn quickly to keep your head down.) In between us is the area called 'no man's land'.

Sometimes when I am feeling low, I have to remind myself why I am here, and how important it is to fight

for people like the Belgians, who did not choose this war.

You know I love animals so I am happy to report that I have a pet. It is a little tabby kitten who strayed in here, and stayed when I tempted her with food. I have named her Lissy to remind me of Lissadell and home (not that I really need reminding!) She's a very sweet little thing. I am sad to say that there are a lot of rats here in the trenches, and Eugene says Lissy will be a great ratter when she's bigger. I'm hoping we'll be home before that happens. I suppose Lissy is French, but she could easily stray away and go and live in a German trench. Maybe cats are smarter than us!

The other big news is that we all got a present of a very nice tin from Princess Mary. The smokers got a tin with cigarettes, but the rest of us got sweets and a pencil and a Christmas card. (That means you are reading a letter written with a pencil from a real princess!). I am going to save the sweets and share them with you girls when I get home. When Eugene opened his tin he said it had a ten pound note in it – and how the other lads went mad

before he told them he was joking!

Everyone got a Christmas card from the King and Queen too and there was a lot of excitement about that.

I hope Christmas is nice and calm and peaceful at Lissadell. I am sorry I won't be there, but I will be thinking of you all the time.

Happy Christmas from your good friend

Harry

* * *

The door opened, casting light from the passageway across my bed.

'Delia? Is that you? Is it morning already? Is it Christmas morning?'

'No,' came a whispered voice as the door closed. 'It's me, Johanna, and it's still Christmas Eve.'

Now Nellie woke too. 'Johanna? What's wrong? Are you sick?'

I could hear Johanna sliding into bed with her

sister. 'No, I'm not sick,' she said. 'But I'm very, very sad. It's Harry. I'm so...' Her sobbing meant I couldn't hear the rest of her words, but I was able to guess them.

'You're worried about him,' I said.

'Yes. He's living in a trench and not far away there's a whole army who'd like to kill him and Eugene and all their friends. It's cold, and they're hungry and there are rats. We're here, safe in our warm beds, with our bellies full of Cook's fine food – it's not fair. None of this is fair.'

I went to lie beside her. The small bed was a bit squashed, but that didn't matter. I wrapped my arms around Johanna, trying to comfort her (and also trying to stop myself from tumbling down onto the hard, cold floor).

'I feel so helpless,' said Johanna. 'All we can do is send him cake and socks and vests.'

'But that must help,' said Nellie. 'He said the socks keep him warm, and the cake is delicious.'

'I know, pet,' said Johanna. 'He's trying to make us feel better. But I've been lying in bed, and every time I close my eyes, all I can think of is my poor Harry, out there in the cold and dark – it breaks my heart, girls. It truly breaks my heart.'

She cried for a while, and I thought my heart would break too from listening to her.

'Shhhh, Johanna,' soothed Nellie. 'Stop crying and try to get some sleep.'

'I can't,' wailed Johanna. 'I'm sorry, but I can't.'

After a while, I knew none of us was getting back to sleep, so I got up and put on the gas light.

'What's that for?' said Nellie, rubbing her eyes.

'There's no point all of us just lying here,' I said. 'We might as well do something useful. Here, Johanna, take my knitting. I'm at the turn of a heel, and you're better than me at that.'

She took my knitting and Nellie pulled hers from under the bed. There was still a spark of life in the fire, so I added a few sticks, and blew on them until

they began to glow, bringing a little more warmth to our room.

'What about you, Lily?' asked Johanna as they began to knit. 'What are you going to do?'

I picked up my book, *Little Women*, and turned to the first page. 'I'm going to take you back to another Christmas, and another war. If we remember we're not the first people to be sad at Christmas, maybe we'll feel the tiniest little bit better.'

And so I began to read. 'Christmas won't be Christmas without any presents…'

I read quietly until I heard the kitchen clock chiming midnight, and the girls dropped their knitting and fell asleep. I put out the gas light and climbed back into my own bed. I looked through the window at the quarter moon, silver and cold in the dark sky over Lissadell. I thought of Harry, so far away. Was he looking at the same moon, and thinking of us?

'Goodnight, girls,' I whispered. 'Good night, Harry and Eugene, wherever you are.'

* * *

It was a Christmas like none I'd ever experienced before. There were presents and blazing fires and fine food and music. Sometimes we laughed, and sometimes we remembered the war, and were sad.

I knew I was lucky to be at Lissadell with good friends like Nellie and Johanna and the other servants, but I missed Mam and my little brothers and sisters.

I missed Harry's warm smile, and the way he told us everything that was happening in the world.

Strangest of all, I missed Maeve, even though she was sleeping under the very same roof as me. Sometimes I saw her, almost like a ghost, flitting along the corridors with her family and the young guests, chatting and laughing and swishing their silk and satin skirts. Often she was just feet away from me, but she was always in another world, one that could never be mine.

Chapter Twenty

*D*ecember 25th 1914

Oh, girls, this will be a long letter, because I have so much to say, and you won't believe the half of it. Yesterday was Christmas Eve and when night came I was feeling very low. I lay in my trench looking up at the moon and thinking of you all, maybe looking at the same moon, but still so very far away. I wanted to eat the last slice of Cook's cake, but then I'd have nothing to look forward to on Christmas Day, so I stopped myself. I was falling off to sleep when Eugene called me. We carefully looked over the top and saw that some of the Germans had put up Christmas trees with candles on them. That made me feel lonelier than ever when I thought of last year's tree at Lissadell, and how happy we all were, with no thought of war at all. Then we heard the sound of singing. It was low at first and became louder as it spread all across the

German trenches. We couldn't understand the words, but we knew the tune and it was 'Silent Night', and I have to say that tears came to my eyes – and I wasn't the only one. When they finished singing we all clapped, as if we were at a concert in the town hall. Then some of our lads started to sing the song in English, and we all joined in. I'm not the best singer in the world, but I sang as loud as I could and for the first time in weeks my loneliness slipped away a little and I felt a moment of joy.

Then we heard some of the Germans calling 'half-way' and at first we didn't understand, but they began to climb out of their trenches and walk into no man's land. Some of our lads walked towards them and at first I stayed where I was, thinking it might be a trap, but then I swear I could not stop myself. I climbed up, pulling Eugene after me, and I ran towards these men, and we shook hands and smiled, and they talked to us in the bits of English they knew. After that we began to show each other our photographs. I wished I had one of you girls, but I showed them the one of Mam and Dad, and a German touched

it and said 'very nice.' Then a German gave me a bar of chocolate, and another one gave me a piece of sausage, and all I had to give was my last slice of Cook's cake, and I was happy to give it on this strange night – and I wonder what she will think about that, if you decide to tell her. And after that we all went back to our own trenches, and Lissy appeared and I put her under my coat to keep her warm and safe, and the only shelling was from very far away, and most of us slept well, with our bellies full of that strange German sausage.

In the morning, it was bright and sunny, but very cold, and the first thing I noticed was how quiet it was – so quiet I could even hear the birds singing and that was a sweet sound I can tell you. After we had our tea to warm up, our lads began to walk into no man's land again, and the Germans did too. Eugene found a German who lived not far from him in London before the war, and they talked about streets where they both walked on their way to work. One of our lads was a barber in his own life, and he set up a chair, and cut hair – even for the Ger-

mans, and they were all laughing, and paying him with food and sweets. Then some lads started a kick-around, though they had no ball, and had to use an old tin, and they put down helmets instead of goalposts. And Eugene and I could never resist a game, so we joined in and Eugene even scored a goal, and he jumped up and down, and for a minute it was as if we were young lads again, back home in Sligo.

The Germans are men just like us with mams and sweethearts, and for a while today we forgot why we're trying to kill each other. But then we were ordered back to our trenches, and that's where I am now, and it is quiet, but I expect that tomorrow we'll be at war again and this day will be like a strange dream in the middle of a long nightmare.

I hope Christmas at Lissadell was warm and happy and peaceful for you all. I hope I'll never again spend a Christmas at war, but for all that, this was a day I'll remember forever - and not in a bad way.

Your friend

Harry

It was a week after Christmas and the guests had all left. My friends and I were sitting on Nellie's bed, and when we finished reading, we could hardly see for the tears.

'Why are we crying?' said Nellie. 'It's a happy letter, isn't it?'

'Of course it's happy,' said Johanna. 'I'm glad Harry's Christmas was so nice. I love his letters, and cannot get them often enough, and yet they make me sad. When I read them I miss him even more. They make me see a little of what he's going through – and that breaks my heart.'

I hugged her. 'Soon the war will be over and he'll come home – and when you're old and grey, the two of you can tell your grandchildren all about Harry's Christmas in France.'

'Lily!' said Johanna, pushing me away, but I could see she was pleased at the thought of growing old

with Harry.

'It's so hard to imagine, though,' said Nellie.

'What is?' I asked.

'How you could be trying to kill someone one minute, and then be able to forget that and be friends – even if it's only for one day.'

'You're right,' said Johanna. 'It just shows that if you try hard enough, you can forgive anything and anyone.'

I jumped up quickly, and grabbed my shawl.

'What are you doing, Lily?' said Nellie.

'I have to go somewhere,' I said, hurrying towards the door.

'But it's the middle of the night,' said Nellie.

'And you're in your nightgown,' said Johanna.

'It doesn't matter,' I said. 'There's something important I have to do – and it can't wait till morning.'

Chapter Twenty-One

The house was quiet, and the tick of the kitchen clock seemed very loud. The worn steps of the servants' stairs were cold under my bare feet, and I pulled my shawl tighter around my shoulders as I hurried up one flight, and then another.

I stepped into the corridor where the family slept and felt my toes sink into the soft, deep rugs. When I saw that no one was around, I hurried to the room I wanted and tapped on the door. At first there was no answer, but when I knocked again, I heard a sleepy voice.

'Who is it? What do you want?'

Instead of answering, I pushed the door open and slipped into the room. The moon was almost full,

casting a trail of silvery light across the floor. The fire had gone out and it was cold.

'It's me, Lily,' I said standing in the middle of the room, not very sure what I was going to do or say next.

'Lily?' said Maeve as she sat up, rubbing her eyes. 'What are you doing here?'

Now I felt a bit foolish.

Was she going to ignore me, or tell me to go away?

Was she going to ring her bell to call some other servant, and make a fuss?

But Maeve didn't do any of these things. 'Is something wrong?' she asked.

There were so many things I wanted to say – but I couldn't find the words for any of them. And then I started to cry.

'What *is* it?' said Maeve, jumping out of bed. 'Lily, please tell me what's happened.'

She took my arm and led me towards the bed, gently pushing me until I was sitting down.

'Harry wrote a letter to Johanna and Nellie and me,' I said. ' ... and there was a truce ... and our soldiers and the Germans were friends for a while ... and they played football even though they were supposed to be enemies ... and, oh, Maeve ... I ... I miss you.'

For a second she didn't react, and I wondered if I'd made a big mistake, but then she too began to cry.

'Lily,' she said. 'I miss you too. I miss you so much.'

She sat beside me and we put our arms around each other, not saying anything.

'It's cold,' said Maeve then, so we got into bed and pulled the blankets over us. The bed was so soft, it was like lying on a cloud, and the blankets were fluffy and warm against my chilly feet. I wanted to close my eyes and float away.

'I want to say sorry to you, Lily,' said Maeve. 'That day ... ages ago ... on your birthday...'

'You don't need to say anything.'

'Please let me. Please let me make things right between us again.'

And she sounded so sad, and so hopeful, I knew I had to listen.

'I know I say stupid, careless things sometimes – like that you could afford a pony – or that you can spend the whole day with me, and not work at all – and I'm sorry if that hurts you.'

'It doesn't really...' I began, but then I stopped myself. How could we be friends if we didn't tell the truth?

'It does hurt a bit,' I said.

'I think it's because ... when you and I are together, I forget about the rest of our lives – I don't think about me being rich and you ... well ... not being rich ... it's just you and me ... two girls, two friends doing nice things together.'

'I understand – and I like the things we do together too.'

'But that day, the day of your birthday, that wasn't me being careless – that day was worse. I knew I was hurting you – but I couldn't stop myself.'

There was no point denying it. 'I know you're not a mean person, Maeve – but what you said that day ... I don't understand it. Why did you talk to me like that?'

'It was the shawl – when I saw your lovely new shawl...'

'But you have so many nice things! And you don't even wear shawls – but if you did, you could have a hundred of them, in every colour of the rainbow.'

'Your mother made it for you.' Her voice was so quiet I could hardly hear the words. 'You've told me how hard she works – and the thought of her knitting late at night, without even a gas light to help her – she must love you so very much.'

At last I began to understand.

'Last year my mother sent me a dress for my birthday,' she said. 'It was a beautiful dress of fine silk and lace.'

'That sounds lovely.'

'It *was* lovely – except it was a dress for a girl much

younger than me. Mother didn't even know what size I was. And this year ... this year she didn't send me anything at all. I waited and waited, and thought it might arrive late, but days and days went by and nothing came. Mother forgot me. She forgot her only girl, and it makes me so sad.'

It made me sad too, but how could I say that? How could I say what I really thought – that Maeve's mother had done a terrible thing?

'I know you feel bad,' I said. 'But your mother believes that what she's doing in Dublin is right.'

'She *is* doing the right thing. I'm proud of her for standing up for what she believes in. I'm proud that she doesn't spend her whole life sitting around doing embroidery and playing the piano. I don't expect her to spend every minute of her time with me, but on my birthday ... on my birthday, all I wanted to know was that she loves me, and hasn't forgotten about me. I wanted to know that I'm her special girl.'

'I've seen you two together, and it's easy to see that

she loves you. I think maybe she loves in a different way to the way my mam loves, or the way Lady Mary does. Your mother doesn't love you less, she just loves you differently.'

'You really think so?'

'I really do,' I said. It was the truth, but it's also true that I'm very happy my mam loves me the way she does, with warm hugs, and special presents, and a sense that everything I do is important to her.

'Thank you, Lily,' said Maeve. 'Now that I've told you this, can you forgive me?'

'Of course I can – and I know you tried to tell me before – but – I'm sorry – I was angry and hurt and I pushed you away – can you forgive me for that?'

'Yes I can – but there's one thing.'

'What?'

'If you call me Miss Maeve again, our friendship will be over forever!'

* * *

Next morning I sang and hummed as I worked. Harry's story of the truce was still running through my head, and Maeve and I were friends again. Life was good – for a few days.

Chapter Twenty-Two

'*N*ellie, Lily, you need to give the drawing room an extra going over today.'

'Yes, Mrs Bailey,' I said. 'Are visitors coming?'

'I don't know if you'd call them visitors,' she said. 'I think it's more of a business meeting with Sir Josslyn – but that's no concern of yours. You two just get on with your jobs.'

She hurried away, just as Isabelle came along the passageway.

'I know who's coming,' said Isabelle. 'I heard Lady Mary and Sir Josslyn talking about it this morning.' Because Isabelle spent most of her time upstairs, she often knew more about the house than Nellie and I did.

'Is it anyone interesting?' asked Nellie.

'They'd need to be *very* interesting to make up for

all the extra work we have to do,' I sighed.

'The visitors will be quite interesting,' said Isabelle. 'Sir Josslyn has offered to help the war effort by setting up a munitions factory in the machine workshop over near the coach house.'

'What's a munitions factory?' asked Nellie.

'It's where they make guns and ammunition,' said Isabelle.

'Guns!' said Nellie, looking shocked.

'They're not actually going to make guns,' said Isabelle. 'They're going to make shell-casings.'

'Sir Josslyn is a farmer,' I said. 'What would he know about shell-casings?'

'It seems his brother Mordaunt works in an engineering firm in England, and he's been giving him advice,' said Isabelle.

'I don't like the idea of such things being made here,' said Nellie. 'How is Johanna going to feel when she hears this? When she hears that Sir Josslyn's going to make shells designed to kill soldiers?'

'I think it's a good thing,' said Isabelle. 'If everyone helps, the war will be over sooner.'

Maybe she was right. I thought of the poor Belgian family I'd met, hunted from their home. I thought about Harry and Eugene, cold and scared in a trench far away. But then I thought of the young German men Harry had written about – the men who shared chocolate, and played football, and sang Christmas songs, and showed photographs of their mothers. Was Sir Josslyn going to be part of their deaths?

I didn't like war, and there were no easy answers. If this munitions factory went ahead, then the war was going to be even closer to us than before.

* * *

Next day, Nellie and I were finished cleaning Lady Mary's bedroom, when I looked out the window and saw a man coming along the drive on a bicycle. I'd never seen him before, but still I felt sorry for him. I

could tell by his shabby suit and bockety bicycle, that he wasn't a rich visitor for the family.

'Look, Nellie,' I said. 'Look at the man out there.'

She came over and looked too, as he leaned his bicycle against the wall, and went towards the *porte cochère*, dusting down his suit as he went.

'Poor man,' she said. 'He must be here about the job in the stables.'

I remembered my first day at Lissadell, when I too had come to the front door, not knowing that people like me were supposed to use the servants' tunnel.

'He's going to be so embarrassed when he realises his mistake,' I said. 'I hope Edward is kind to him. Let's go and watch.'

We gathered our mops and brushes and hurried along the corridor towards the main stairs.

'We shouldn't be here,' said Nellie as I stopped half way down. 'What if someone sees us?'

'If anyone comes along, we can pretend we're sweeping.'

Nellie, who wasn't very good at telling lies, actually began to sweep the already clean stairs. We watched as Edward opened the door, stepping back in surprise when he saw the stranger. We couldn't hear what was said, but a second later, the man was standing in the hallway, holding his cap in one hand, and using the other to flatten down his greying hair. Edward hurried towards the dining room, looking worried. This was very strange.

Soon, Lady Mary came along. She shook the man's hand, and led him to the small room off the hallway. They went inside, and the door closed behind them.

'Who can he be?' I said.

'I don't care,' said Nellie. 'Let's go, Lily. I don't want to be caught lurking here. We'll get in trouble.'

'Don't worry. It'll be...' I couldn't finish, as Sir Josslyn came across the hall and up the stairs. Nellie and I were both a bit afraid of him, so we gathered our buckets and hurried down to the basement.

A little while later Nellie and I went back upstairs to clean Maeve's bedroom.

'I'm so glad you and Maeve are friends again,' she said, as we shook out the last of the blankets.

'Me too – but she's going to Ardeevin today, and I'll miss her.'

The door opened. 'Maeve,' I said as I turned around. 'When do you think you'll be...?'

But I stopped talking. It wasn't Maeve at the door. It was Mrs Bailey – and she looked very serious. Were Nellie and I in trouble? Had Sir Josslyn told her about us hanging around the stairs, trying to eavesdrop?

I turned to Nellie who looked ready to cry, and felt bad. *I* was the one who'd insisted on listening. Would Mrs Bailey believe me if I said it was all my fault?

'We're almost finished here, Mrs Bailey,' I said as brightly as I could.

'You're needed downstairs in the servants' dining hall – both of you.'

'Yes, Mrs Bailey,' I said. 'We just have to sweep here and then...'

'Now!' said Mrs Bailey. 'Leave that and go downstairs immediately.'

As we headed for the back stairs, with Mrs Bailey following us, poor Nellie looked terrified. I smiled trying to make her feel a little better, but she didn't smile back

As we went down the stairs in silence, one thing confused me. Mrs Bailey was very stern and serious, but she didn't seem angry. If Nellie and I were in so much trouble, why wasn't Mrs Bailey cross with us?

* * *

I opened the door of the dining hall, and stopped in surprise – the room was almost full, though it wasn't even close to dinner time. Most of the servants were

standing there, looking worried. Whatever was going on, I now knew it had nothing to do with Nellie and me eavesdropping on the stairs – this had to be something worse.

Nellie and I hurried over to stand next to Johanna.

'What's going on?' I whispered.

'I don't know,' she said. 'No one seems to know anything.'

'Maybe it's something to do with yesterday's visitors?' I suggested. 'Maybe they need some of us to work in the munitions factory.'

'*I* wouldn't like that,' said Nellie.

'Neither would I,' I said. 'I like my jobs in the sewing school and the nursery – and even cleaning fireplaces would be better than making ammunition.'

Mr Kilgallon appeared, and any whispering stopped as he went to the top of the room and stood next to Mrs Bailey.

'Lady Mary has had a visitor this morning,' he said. 'It was Harry's father. I thought it best to tell you all,

as I know Harry is very dear to many of you.'

Next to me, Johanna gasped. I turned to see that her face had gone whiter than the wall behind her. I held my hand towards her, and she took it, squeezing so hard I thought she'd grind my bones to dust.

'Last night Harry's father had a telegram,' continued Mr Kilgallon.

I wanted to shut my eyes and cover my ears. Poor people like us never got telegrams with good news in them.

'It was bad news,' said Mr Kilgallon. 'Harry went missing in action on New Year's Day, somewhere in France.'

At these words, the whispering began again, and behind me I could hear someone crying. Luckily Johanna was still holding my hand, as I just managed to grab her as her knees went from under her. Nellie helped me get her sister to a bench, where she sat for a moment, with a strange wild look in her eyes. Then she bent her head to her hands and began to cry. 'My

Harry,' she wailed. 'My lovely Harry is gone.'

I stroked her hair and tried to calm her. 'He's only missing,' I said.

'Missing isn't too bad, Jojo,' said Nellie. 'Missing means we can still hope. Missing might mean Harry's still alive, and that he'll be able to come back to us.'

But nothing we could say seemed to help. Poor Johanna sat between us and cried in a way I'd never heard anyone cry before. So Nellie and I sat beside her, and held her hands, and didn't even try to hold back our own tears.

After a while, Mr Kilgallon clapped his hands and the whispering stopped.

'All we can do is hope and pray that Harry is found, and will come back to us safely. I understand that this is upsetting news, so you may all take half an hour off, and after that you must return to your work.'

Mrs Bailey came over to where we were sitting. She patted Johanna's back gently, but Johanna didn't look up. 'I know you girls were very close to Harry,' said

Mrs Bailey. 'And I can only imagine how upset you must be. Despite what Mr Kilgallon says, I think we can manage without you three for the rest of the day.'

I stared at her, wiping away my tears. Normally, the idea of a surprise day off would have had me dancing for joy, but now I felt as if a huge cloud had settled over us, and was never going to lift. I wished this was a normal day, with hours of cleaning ahead of me.

'What should we do?' asked Nellie.

'Take Johanna to your room, and let her lie down for a little while,' said Mrs Bailey. 'I'll send Delia in with some sweet tea for the three of you.'

Tea in our room should have been a big treat, but all I wished was for time to go backwards. I wished Harry's dad had never appeared at Lissadell.

I wished Harry had never gone to war.

I wished he was safe here, telling jokes, ironing the newspapers and keeping us up to date with what was going on in the world.

I wanted everything to be different.

Chapter Twenty-Three

*J*ohanna spent the rest of that day in our room. She wouldn't talk, or eat any of the food Cook sent in for us. I tried to eat a little, but everything tasted like dry and dusty cardboard.

After a while Johanna stopped crying, and lay on Nellie's bed, silent and pale and sad. That night she slept curled up in Nellie's arms, but often I woke to hear her sobbing in the cool darkness.

I woke early the next morning – so early, the basement was still quiet. Johanna and Nellie were sleeping. At last Johanna looked peaceful, and I dreaded the moment she would wake, and the terrible truth would come to her once again.

* * *

A few days later, Mrs Bailey came to find Nellie and me.

'Stop what you're doing and go downstairs immediately,' she said.

'What is it?' I asked. 'Is there news of Harry?'

'It's Johanna,' said Mrs Bailey. 'She needs you. You will find her in her room.'

* * *

Johanna was lying on her bed, sobbing. Nellie threw herself down beside her sister, and stroked her hair.

'Tell us what's wrong?' I said. 'Is it Harry?'

Instead of answering, Johanna held out the letter that was crumpled in her hand.

'It's from Harry,' she said.

Nellie sat up. 'That's great news. You've had all that upset for nothing. You'll have to write him a cross letter for making us worry like that.'

But I didn't understand. I know that sometimes

people cry when they're happy – but Johanna's tears didn't look like happy ones.

'Johanna,' I said quietly. 'Why are you crying?'

She sat up and looked at me with her puffy, red eyes.

'Look at the date on the letter,' she said. 'He wrote it just after Christmas ... before ... before ...'

'Before he went missing,' I said. 'Telegrams go faster than letters, don't they?'

She nodded, and held the letter towards me again. 'You can read it.'

'Is it for Nellie and me too?'

'No – but you can read it anyway.'

So I took the letter, and read it aloud.

December 29th 1914

Dearest Johanna,

I'm sad to say that once Christmas day was over, the truce was well and truly forgotten, and there has been some very fierce fighting. At first it was strange, seeing

those nice lads as our enemies again.

This is going to be a short letter, as we are advancing tomorrow and there's a lot to do — but if I don't write now, I don't know when I'll get the chance again. No time to write to Nellie and Lily, so please give them my best regards.

Johanna, you are the sweetest girl in the world, and I am a lucky man to know you. I cannot wait for the day I see your smiling eyes again.

Try not to worry too much. Me and Eugene are hardy Sligo lads, and will look after each other.

Must go now.

All my love

Your Harry

I handed the letter to Johanna, and she folded it carefully and put it back in the envelope.

'That might be the last letter I'll get from Harry,' she said. 'Those might be the last words I'll ever hear from him.'

* * *

The next few days and weeks passed very slowly.

Nellie and I worked hard as usual, and also tried to take care of Johanna, who wandered the house, looking like a ghostly shadow of herself. At night she lay in our room, though I doubt she slept very much, as in the morning her face was always pale, and she had huge dark shadows under her eyes. She can't have been any good as a lady's maid, but Lady Mary never complained, and was always gentle and kind with her.

As I worked I kept an eye on the driveway, though I wasn't sure if I wanted to see Harry's dad. If he came to see Lady Mary again, would that be good news, or...?

After all the meetings, it was decided that the munitions factory wouldn't be set up for a while, and I was glad to hear it. How would poor Johanna feel if she had to watch ammunition leaving Lissadell, for

the war that might have taken the man she loved?

* * *

Then one morning, when Delia knocked on the door to wake us, Johanna opened her eyes, sat up and stretched.

'Time to get up, girls,' she said brightly. 'You don't want to be getting in trouble with Mrs Bailey.'

As Nellie rolled over and struggled to wake, I turned to Johanna. 'Are you ... are you all right?' I asked.

'Thank you, Lily, I am very well.'

For a moment, I wondered if she had somehow managed to forget about Harry being missing. Had she wiped away the memory to protect herself? Would I have to tell her about it all over again?

But then she smiled. 'I'm sorry I've been making such a fuss,' she said. 'It must have been upsetting for you both.'

'Don't say sorry for that,' I said. 'You heard that...'

'I heard that Harry is missing,' she said. 'But I must have faith in him. Wherever he is, I know he'll come back to us.'

Nellie hugged her. 'Eugene will find him,' she said.

'And when he gets back, Harry will laugh at us for being so worried,' said Johanna.

I stared at her, not sure what to say.

'Don't you see, Lily?' said Johanna. 'For years I thought Nellie had died in the workhouse. I gave up hope – and that was a terrible thing. But in the end I was wrong. She was alive and well and waiting for me. So I'm not giving up on Harry. I *can't* give up on him. I believe he's coming back to Lissadell, and to me.'

I wished I could feel as certain as she did, but how could I argue? How could I take away any hope she had left?

So we all got dressed and did our best to get on with our normal day.

* * *

In the evenings after that, Johanna knitted furiously, barely stopping to eat or talk. She wrote long letters to Harry, and encouraged Nellie and me to do the same. I didn't want to upset her, so I did as she asked, though it seemed strange.

I felt weak and helpless. Sometimes I wished I could join the army, and go to France or Belgium and search for our friend. It seemed cruel that all we girls could do was sit in our rooms, and knit socks that might never be worn, and write letters that might never be read.

Chapter Twenty-Four

'See Lily, it's all done,' said Hugh.

I took the slate from him. 'Look at that!' I said. 'Aren't you a great little boy altogether.'

The letters he'd copied were a bit crooked, and the d's and b's were facing the wrong way, but I could see he'd done his very best. I gave him more work to do and went to check on Michael who was doing sums at the desk by the window. Michael smiled shyly at me, and I had to resist the urge to give him a big hug. He was so quiet and serious all the time.

I loved working in the schoolroom with these two sweet boys, and wished I could spend more time there. I spun the globe gently, thinking about all the geography and history I'd like to teach them. If I was a teacher I'd be happy to work day and night, while every minute of being a housemaid felt like a hun-

dred years.

As I tidied up the room for the end of the lesson, I was surprised when the door opened.

'Lady Mary,' I said, as Hugh ran to her for a hug.

'Hello, darling boys,' she said. 'Off you go back to the nursery. I need to have a word with Lily.'

Michael and Hugh did as they were told, and when they were gone, Lady Mary turned to me.

'I want to say that you've been doing an excellent job with the boys,' she said. 'They both love your lessons and are coming on in leaps and bounds. You truly are an excellent teacher, Lily.'

For a minute I dared to hope.

Was she going to say she had decided not to employ a tutor after all?

Had she decided I was such a good teacher I could do the job as well as any man who went to some fancy university far away?

Could I teach the boys all day long, until they were old enough for boarding school?

And later could I continue with Bridget and Brian, and even little Rosaleen?

Maybe Lady Mary could keep on having babies, and I could teach them forever, and never have to clean a fireplace or scrub a floor again?

But then she continued to speak. 'I have interviewed a tutor, and he will be arriving in a few weeks' time – so after that you can go back to your normal duties. I'm sure the tutor will be pleasantly surprised when he sees how much you have taught the boys.'

She said lots more, and I continued to nod politely, but I couldn't really pay attention, as I watched my dreams vanish like dust in the wind.

* * *

When Lady Mary finally left, I stayed in the schoolroom for a few minutes, picking up the last of the chalk, and the coloured wooden bricks Hugh had been using for counting. I did this slowly, delaying

the moment I'd have to go back downstairs, to my normal work.

I heard a sound outside, and I was afraid it was Lady Mary again, and I wondered if I'd be able to continue my fake smiling and nodding. When the door opened, and Maeve skipped in, I couldn't help myself – I put my head in my hands and began to cry.

'What is it, Lily?' she said putting her arm around me. 'Why are you crying? Have you had news of Harry?'

I shook my head, feeling foolish. 'No – it's not about Harry – and while he's missing, I shouldn't be crying about anything else.'

'You're allowed to be sad,' she said, putting her arm around me. 'Tell me what's wrong.'

So I told her why I was crying. 'I can see why you're disappointed,' she said when I was finished.

'I've no right to be,' I said. 'Lady Mary told me from the start that I'd only be teaching the boys for a little while – only, I let myself hope, and...'

'You poor girl. It doesn't seem fair. I've seen how good you are with my cousins, though I don't know how you do it – they can be very annoying.' Then she gave a big smile. 'I've got a great idea,' she said. 'When the tutor arrives, we can find a way to get rid of him. We could put slugs in his bed, or fill his pockets with rotten eggs.'

I smiled too, feeling a bit better knowing she was on my side. 'Thank you, Maeve, but I don't think that's a good idea. You and I would get in trouble, and Lady Mary would simply hire another tutor.'

'Maybe you're right. Anyway, I came to see if you'd like to walk down to the beach with me? Mrs Bailey says she can spare you for an hour.'

'Thank you,' I said. 'I'd like that.' And I set off with my friend.

* * *

On Saturday I went home as usual, feeling free as

I cycled along the quiet roads, with the wind in my hair and the cold bright sun in my eyes.

Mam was in the front yard when I arrived, and I jumped off the bike and into her arms.

'Ah, my darling girl,' she said, when I clung on to her for even longer than usual.

'Thanks, Mam,' I said when I finally let her go. 'I've been waiting for that hug for a whole week.'

'Well then here's another one for good measure,' she said, throwing her arms around me again, and squeezing me tight. 'Now come inside before we all freeze to death.'

We went inside and sat by the fire, with Winnie and Anne cuddled up beside us, while Denis and Jimmy examined my basket to see what treats Cook had sent for us.

'So tell me,' said Mam. 'Is there any news of your friend, Harry?'

'No,' I said. 'Not another word. It's so sad for Johanna – and for the rest of us too. We don't know

what's happened, and we're trying to be hopeful, but it's hard. Wherever he is, surely he'd be able to write to us – wouldn't he?'

'Maybe he's in a hospital somewhere. He could be injured – unconscious even?'

'Oh, Mam, I wish Harry never went away to war. I wish he was still safe at Lissadell with us.'

'It's not easy, but many people think he did the right thing,' she said. 'Did you hear that more refugees have been arriving in Ireland all week? And there are terrible stories coming from France and Belgium. I don't know if war is ever right, but in this case it's hard to argue.'

We talked for a while, and Mam did her best, but in the end, even she couldn't make me feel better. If Harry didn't come back...

* * *

I was at the very edge of the village, on my way back

to Lissadell, when I heard a deep gruff voice that sounded familiar.

'Lily Brennan – is that you?'

I pulled the brakes and skidded on the gravel, nearly falling on top of The Master, my teacher from the village school.

'I'm so sorry, Sir,' I said. 'I didn't see you – and it's hard to stop when I'm going fast and...'

I stopped talking, feeling foolish. I knew my face was red, and my hair was blown all over the place, making me look like a wild girl.

He laughed. 'Always drama when you're around, Lily,' he said. 'I'm glad to see that hasn't changed. I hear you've been teaching the young Gore-Booth children.'

'I have, but how...?' Then I realised. 'You met Mam, didn't you?'

He smiled. 'She's very proud of you – and rightly so. I remember well how good you were with the little ones when you were at school with us – you

were a grand little teacher.'

'Thank you,' I said. 'But the Gore-Booths are getting a tutor, so I'm not a teacher any more. Sometimes I help in the sewing school, but mostly I'm back to being a housemaid again.'

'Miss O'Brien is stepping out with a man from Donegal these days.'

I wondered why he was suddenly talking about Miss O'Brien, the other teacher from my old school.

'That's interesting,' I said. 'But...'

'They have recently become engaged, and sooner or later they will be married. When that happens, Miss O'Brien will be moving to his home place – and there will be a vacancy in the school. Maybe by then you...?'

The red had been fading from my face, but now it came back again. The Master was being kind, but what was he thinking? He'd seen the poor small cottage I grew up in. He'd seen my mam, struggling to feed and clothe us. He'd seen my brothers who some-

times didn't have a pair of shoes between them.

'Thank you,' I said. 'But I can't afford to be a teacher – Mam hasn't got the money to send me to college, and I could never save up enough either.'

'There is another way, you know.'

'There is?'

'There's a thing called a Junior Assistant Mistress – or JAM for short. Have you heard of this?'

I shook my head.

'Well, JAMs work with the junior classes – they teach all subjects to the little children, and teach singing, cookery and needlework to the older girls too.'

I sighed. 'I'd wake up happy every day of my life if that was my job.'

'The interesting thing is that JAMs don't have any formal training. They only need a good standard of primary education – and I can vouch for the fact that you've had that.'

'So does that mean...?'

I was too excited to finish the sentence.

'You're a bit young yet, but in a year's time you'd be plenty old enough. Why don't you and your mam come to talk to me the next time you're home – and maybe we can discuss this some more?'

'Oh, Sir!' I could feel tears coming to my eyes, and wiped them away quickly. If the Master thought I was a big baby, maybe he'd change his mind. 'Oh, Sir,' I said again. 'Thank you so much. I won't let you down. I promise I won't.'

He laughed his deep, warm laugh. 'I'll expect to see you and your mam very soon. Now off you go, or you'll be out too late.'

* * *

The journey back to Lissadell seemed to take no time at all, as I pedalled like the wind, with wild, happy thoughts racing around my head.

I stopped for a minute when Lissadell House came

into view. I remembered my very first day there, when everything seemed so strange and new and frightening.

When I didn't know a single soul inside those grey walls.

When I was afraid of all those strangers.

When I thought I was going to be working there for the rest of my days.

I jumped back on my bike, and raced on. I had to tell my friends the great news. They would all be so happy for me. I had to tell Nellie and Johanna and Maeve. I had to tell Harry, who always encouraged me to follow my dream.

And then I remembered. Harry wasn't there.

Chapter Twenty-Five

'Hello, Mrs Bailey,' said Maeve with a big smile on her face. 'I wonder if Lily...?'

The housekeeper gave a big sigh as she turned to me. 'One hour and no more. If you're not back by three o'clock...'

'I will be, I promise,' I said, as I hurried to put my sweeping brush away. 'Thank you Mrs Bailey.'

'I got you a present, Lily,' said Maeve.

I took the small package. 'Thank you, but why...?'

'It's to say sorry, for ... before...'

'There's no need,' I stopped talking as I opened the package and saw the adorable brooch in the shape of a seal.

'Oh, Maeve,' I sighed. 'It's gorgeous, but it's too

much. I've never had ... I can't take ... well, maybe ... it's so lovely! It reminds me of Spotty the seal who was little Michael's pet last year ... I ...'

Maeve took the brooch and pinned it to my apron. It looked lovely, but immediately I began to worry.

'Don't worry,' she said. 'There are probably rules about you wearing jewellery on your uniform, but you can wear it now, with me, and after that you can save it for when you're going home.'

'Thank you,' I said. 'Thank you for the present, and for understanding.'

'You're welcome,' she said, taking my hand. 'Let's walk to the stables and see Star.'

'Good idea.' I didn't care where Maeve wanted to go. It was a lovely day, and an hour outside sounded like heaven on earth.

As we walked I told Maeve all about my meeting with the Master.

'So you're really going to be a teacher, Lily,' she said. 'I'll miss you very much if you leave Lissadell,

but I'm so happy your dream is coming true.'

'Thank you, but nothing is decided yet. I haven't even had a chance to tell Mam. And I like Miss O'Brien, but she can be very cranky – if her boy-friend realises this, he might decide not to marry her, and she'll stay teaching with the Master until her dying day.'

'If she and her sweetheart break up, you let me know – I'll find a way to get them back together, whether they like it or not.'

'Would that be fair?'

'Who cares? This is your future happiness we're talking about.'

We both laughed.

'There's one other thing though,' I said.

'What?'

'I don't know if I should tell you – it's a bit stupid.'

Maeve stopped walking, 'I'm your friend,' she said. 'So if you want to tell me something, it doesn't matter if you think it's stupid.'

'I very much want to be teacher, but ... sometimes I think I can make a deal with the world.'

'What kind of deal?'

'If I give up on my dream, then maybe Harry could come back.'

For a minute she didn't say anything.

'See,' I said. 'I told you it was stupid.'

'No!' she said fiercely. 'It's not stupid at all. You've dreamed of being a teacher for most of your life, and to think you'd give that up so ...'

'I wouldn't even think twice, if I thought the world worked like that. Oh, Maeve, Nellie and I miss Harry so much, but still, sometimes we forget. Sometimes we laugh, or hum or skip along the corridor. Sometimes a whole hour goes by and I don't think of him at all.'

'There's nothing wrong with that.'

'Maybe not – but the thing is, Johanna never forgets, not even for one single second. She's made so many socks, I can't keep count of them anymore. She

says she believes Harry is safe somewhere, trying to come back to us.'

'If that makes her feel better...'

'I don't think it does. Sometimes when I look at her, I can see she's ready to cry. Sometimes she watches when Edward brings the post downstairs, and she looks terrified. If Harry doesn't come back, I don't think she'd ever get over it. I think she'd mourn him for the rest of her life.'

'That's so sad – but maybe she's right. Maybe he is safe somewhere. Maybe he will return to us.'

'Maybe he will.'

But I wasn't sure I believed this – and as each day passed slowly by, I believed it even less.

* * *

Cook's face was red and she looked about ready to kill someone. 'Where has Ita got to?' she said. 'Why is she never here when I need her?'

I smiled. Ita, the scullery maid, was always tired and was very good at sidling into quiet corners and having quick little naps.

'Maybe she's doing a job for Mrs Bailey,' I said.

Cook looked doubtful. 'Lily, would you be a pet and go to the kitchen garden and get me two big cabbages?'

'Of course, Cook,' I said. She was always kind to me, so I was happy to do her a favour – and anyway, I loved going outside to the fresh, clean air.

'Good girl,' she said handing me a basket and a small knife. 'Be sure to get two of the big dark ones – and put on your coat or you'll catch your death of cold.'

As I went to get my coat, I saw that Johanna's door was open. Inside, I could see her sitting on her bed, knitting furiously as usual.

'Are you all right?' I asked from the doorway.

'I'm fine.' She didn't look fine. Her skin was a greyish colour and there were huge dark circles

under her eyes.

'Why are you here at this time of day?'

'Lady Mary has gone to Sligo Town to meet the refugee committee,' she said. 'So I have a few hours to myself.'

'Why don't you come outside with me? I'm only going to pick some cabbages, so it won't be much fun – but the fresh air will be nice.'

'Thank you, but I'll stay here. I'm nearly finished another pair.' She held up her knitting proudly, making me want to cry.

'If you're sure?'

She nodded, and I left her to her work.

* * *

There were only two cabbages left in the kitchen garden. I picked both quickly, and put them into the basket. Cook was right, it was very cold, but the sun was shining, and I dawdled as I made my way back to

the house. In my daydream, I was a Junior Assistant Mistress, and I had brought the children outside, to teach them about flowers and birds. We were all sitting under a huge tree, and they were begging me for a story, and they were so sweet and...

Far away, I could see a man coming along the driveway on a bicycle, and I felt a sudden chill.

Was this Harry's father?

Was it good news or bad news?

I wanted to run away, and pretend I hadn't seen him.

If it was bad news, I didn't want to be the one to hear it first.

How could I tell Nellie?

How could I tell Johanna?

I didn't want to know.

But it was too late. The man had seen me, and was cycling slowly in my direction. He was wearing a big woolly hat, and strange dark glasses.

I stood, hardly daring to move, as he came closer.

And then...

'Harry?'

I dropped my basket, and the cabbages rolled away down the hill, and into the stream, and set off on a journey that would surely take them to the sea.

I began to run.

'Harry? Is that you?'

He got off his bicycle and let it drop onto the grass. He stood looking back along the driveway, almost as if he too wanted to run away, back out of Lissadell.

'Harry!' I said again in a voice I hardly recognised, not sure if I was crying or laughing. And still he stood there, even as I ran and threw my arms around him. He patted my back.

'Oh, Lily,' he said in the end. 'I thought I would never make it home. I thought I'd never see any of you again.'

I pulled away, but still he wouldn't look at me, as he kept his face half-turned.

'Harry,' I said, dancing around him. 'What's wrong?

248

Why won't you...?'

And then I saw it. One side of his face was perfect, but the other side ... oh, it was terrible to see. His cheek was all cut and scarred and the bottom of his ear was missing. The dark glasses covered his eyes, and I didn't dare to think what they were hiding.

I tried to smile as if nothing was wrong. It was hard to look at him. It was hard not to appear shocked.

'Everyone's going to be so happy to see you,' I said. 'Did you know you were reported as missing? We were all afraid that...'

'I know. My parents told me when I got back this morning, and that's why I came straight here. I'm sorry everyone was so worried about me.'

'But where were you all this time? Why didn't you write to us?'

'I was in a hospital in France. I was unconscious for most of the time, and raving for the rest. It was weeks before they got any good out of me. Until then no one knew who I was, so...'

'Well, you're back now, and that's the important thing,' I said. 'Come on in. Johanna is surely going to die from happiness. Your room is just the way you left it so you'll be able to settle right in. Nellie has missed you too, and everyone has really. We all...'

I forgot about Cook's cabbages and started to walk towards the kitchen, but Harry didn't follow me.

'What is it?' I said. 'You *have* to come in. I'll be killed if people think I was trying to keep you all to myself.'

'I won't be staying.'

I didn't understand. 'Why won't you be staying? You don't mean that ... that you have to go back to the war?'

'No, it's not that.' He pointed at his dark glasses. 'I've lost the sight in one eye, so I can't go back any more, whether I want to or not. No one wants a half-blind soldier.'

'Well that's a relief – oh sorry – I don't mean about your eye ... but ...'

He gave a small laugh, and for the first time I got a sense that this was the same man who had left us just a few months earlier. But then his smile faded, and he seemed like a stranger again.

'I won't be working here anymore.'

'But Sir Josslyn promised!'

'I know. But that was different. That was before ... this.' He waved his hand over the injured side of his face.

'Sir Josslyn won't care about that.'

'I can't hold him to his promise. How can I answer the door to guests looking like this? How can I serve at table?'

'No one will care,' I said. 'Or they might a little bit at first, but then they'll get used to it.'

I wasn't even lying. After only a few minutes, his face didn't seem so strange at all. But Harry didn't believe me.

'I've come to explain to Sir Josslyn,' he said. 'Then I'm going to take my remaining belongings and go

back to my parents' house.'

'But what about Johanna?'

'Johanna can't see me like this.'

'But she loves you. She loves the real you – your face won't matter to her. All she wants is to see you again.'

He shook his head sadly. 'Johanna deserves someone who looks ... not like this.'

'You don't know that. Why don't you ask her?'

'I can't do that. She is a sweet, kind girl – and I don't want her to stay with me out of pity. She needs to forget all about me, and one day she'll meet someone else, someone good enough for her.'

I couldn't see his eyes through the dark glasses, but it sounded as if he might be crying.

'So you're just going to leave without seeing her?'

'It's the best way. I'll leave a note for her – to try to explain.'

'But that's not...'

We were interrupted by the sound of hoof beats

coming along the driveway, and turned to see Sir Josslyn, who stopped his horse next to us.

'There you are, Harry!' he said. 'I have just been to visit your parents, and they told me the great news. It's so good to see you back, safe and...' he stopped, looking embarrassed, and I felt sorry for poor Harry. Was the rest of his life going to be like this – with people staring and saying careless things, and then apologising?

But Sir Josslyn was a gentleman, and he recovered quickly. 'Does that hurt?' he asked, pointing at Harry's injured face.

'It hurt a bit at first,' said Harry bravely. 'But not so much now. The doctors and nurses in France took great care of me.'

'And when do you think you will be well enough to return to work with us?' asked Sir Josslyn.

'I am well now,' said Harry. 'Or at least as well as I'll ever be. But I'm not suitable to be a footman any more. I have come to collect my things, and to thank

you and Lady Mary for your kindness to me in the past.'

Sir Josslyn sighed. 'Your mother told me you have some foolish notion like this – and I'd like to knock that on the head right this minute. You are part of the Lissadell household, and we are all looking forward to having you back with us. Maybe on Monday next – so you'll have a few days to spend with your family and get used to civilian life again?'

I could see Harry wanted to protest, but he was too used to taking orders from Sir Josslyn.

'Yes, Sir,' he said. 'Thank you, Sir.'

'I'll see you on Monday, then,' said Sir Josslyn. 'Please go into the house, and tell Cook I said she's to give you the finest meal she can produce. I know what army rations are like, so I'm sure you need feeding up.'

He clicked his heels, and his horse bucked a little and then galloped off.

'I should go back home,' said Harry. 'Now that

things are settled with Sir Josslyn.'

'No!' I said quickly. 'You heard what he said. You're to have a meal first.'

'All right,' he said. 'But I'm not talking to Johanna.'

The poor man looked terrified. I thought how brave he was to go to war, and live in a trench, and survive a terrible injury – and how strange it was that seeing the girl he loved frightened him so much.

Harry picked up his bicycle and wheeled it along beside me as we walked slowly back to the house.

Chapter Twenty-Six

We stopped at the side door to the kitchen, and Harry propped the bicycle against the wall. I opened the door and stepped inside, but he hesitated, breathing deeply.

'This is so...'

'What?'

'All those weeks, when I was in the trenches – sometimes I could hardly picture this place any more. It was almost as if I had dreamed it up.' He slapped the whitewashed wall beside him. 'And yet here it is – as real and solid as ever – and I'm back.'

'Yes, Harry,' I said. 'You're back.'

'My dear brother is still out there, and I pray every night he'll come home safe to us.'

I'd never met Eugene, but after Harry's letters, he seemed like a friend. I shivered as I thought of him far away, cold and wet and scared and missing his brother.

'Come along,' I said, but still Harry didn't follow me, and I could see he was afraid.

'I won't stay long,' he said. 'I'll eat quickly and be on my way. Will you please tell Nellie and Johanna that I'm not missing any more, that I'm safe? Please tell Johanna that I'll write to her tonight, and explain everything.'

I didn't answer. Harry had worked at Lissadell for a long time, so he knew exactly who was where at any given time.

He knew that Cook would be in the kitchen, panicking about the dinner, even though she would have most of it ready by now.

He knew that Mr Kilgallon would be in his office, doing his weekly accounts.

He knew that Nellie would be cleaning the main

stairs or the bedroom corridor.

He knew that at this time, Johanna should be upstairs, helping Lady Mary to choose her clothes for the afternoon, and for dinner.

He did not know that Lady Mary had gone to Sligo, so Johanna was in her room, only a few feet away, knitting socks for a man she thought was hundreds of miles away – or worse.

'Come on, Harry,' I said. 'Let's go inside. I'm frozen half to death – and I need you to explain to Cook how I managed to lose the last two cabbages in Lissadell.'

* * *

The basement passageway was dark and unusually quiet. I held Harry's hand as we walked towards the kitchen, almost as if he were a trophy I had won, and wanted to show off to my friends.

Then Ita came along towards us, carrying a large bucket of steaming hot water. She stopped when she

saw Harry and her mouth fell open.

She dropped the bucket with a big clatter and didn't seem to care that the water sloshed around all of our feet. Then a huge smile spread across her face.

'Harry!' she shrieked, as she ran back towards the kitchen. 'Harry is back.'

Further along the corridor, Johanna's door flew open and she stepped out. She was barefoot, and her gorgeous red hair was tumbling down around her shoulders. The little colour she'd had before drained away from her face, and now she looked like a very frail, beautiful ghost. She took a step towards us, and stopped and held on to the wall, almost as if her legs were too weak to hold her up.

A second later she took another step, but Harry held up his hand to stop her.

'No,' he said. 'No, Johanna. I am broken. I am not good enough for you.'

Now she came right up to him. When she saw his damaged face, she stopped as if someone had hit her

– but she didn't look away.

'Don't look,' said Harry. 'Please don't look at me.'

But Johanna ignored his words and held her palm near his face, almost, but not quite touching the angry red scars.

'You poor man,' she said. 'What have they done to you?'

Instead of answering, he half turned away. 'You must forget me, Johanna.'

'Harry,' she whispered. 'I'll *never* forget you. I don't care about any of this. You are all I want.'

He shook his head, as if he couldn't bear to hear the words. 'How will I stand it when you look at my ruined face with those perfect blue eyes? All I will see is pity, and that would surely break my heart.'

'Pity, my hat!' she said. 'When I see that face I will love you even more. Every day I'll look at you and remember how you suffered for other people. Every day I'll thank my lucky stars that a fine man like you chose me.'

'But...'

'I'm telling the truth, and if you keep talking that old nonsense about pity, I'll be so angry you'll feel as if you're facing a hundred armies.'

Now the dark glasses couldn't hide the tears that were pouring down Harry's face, though they looked all blurry, as I was crying too.

Harry held out his hands and Johanna took them in hers, and rubbed them as if she could rub away all the pain and hurt of the last few months.

'Johanna,' he whispered over and over again. 'My dear, lovely Johanna.'

I could hear the clump of heavy boots thumping down the stairs. 'Harry!' shrieked Nellie, appearing in a blur of mops and dusters and brushes. 'You're back! I knew it. I knew you'd be back. Johanna, Harry is back.'

'I noticed, dear Nellie,' said Johanna, smiling at her little sister.

Cook came from the kitchen, wiping tears from

her face with a dishcloth. Close behind her were Ita and the kitchen maids, and the commotion brought Mr Kilgallon and Mrs Bailey from their offices. A second later, Maeve appeared, with Isabelle on her heels.

It was very crowded in the small passageway with everyone crying and laughing and talking at the same time. In the middle of us all stood Harry and Johanna, holding hands and smiling at each other as if there was no one else around them, as if there was no one else in the world.

* * *

After a while, when Harry had tried to answer hundreds of questions at the same time, Mr Kilgallon clapped his hands, and the excited chattering stopped.

'Now, everyone,' he said.' We're all very happy to see our dear Harry back, but the man needs food, and rest, and some peace and quiet. Johanna, bring

him into the dining hall, and sit him down. And the rest of you, take twenty minutes to calm yourselves and then get back to your work. Harry will be staying with us, and there will be plenty of time for questions later.'

Johanna and Harry did as they were told, while everyone else drifted away, chatting excitedly about the return of our friend.

Soon only Maeve, Nellie and I were left in the suddenly quiet and ordinary passageway, standing there, not quite sure what to do.

'I'm going to my room,' said Nellie suddenly. 'We've got twenty minutes and I don't want to waste them. I've got socks to knit.'

'But Harry's home,' said Maeve. 'He doesn't...

'Eugene's still out there,' said Nellie. 'And he must be lonely without his brother at his side. The least I can do is send him some warm socks – and maybe a vest or two as well.'

I smiled. We'd already sent enough socks to keep

a whole regiment warm, but my dear, kind friend wanted to help the soldiers any way she could.

'I have an idea,' said Maeve. 'We've got twenty minutes – or maybe more, as I don't think anyone will be cross with us on a day like today. There's a darling litter of kittens in the stables, so why don't the three of us run over and play with them? Then tonight, I'll come to your room, and you can teach me how to knit socks, and we'll knit away and talk and sing and be happy.'

I looked at Nellie, who nodded enthusiastically, so my dear friends and I held hands as we stepped out into the sunshine.

A Note on the History in this Book

Maeve de Markievicz and her family were real people and the Gore-Booth family really did live in Lissadell House at the time this book is set. Though I have strayed a little from the exact truth from time to time, so the story could flow more freely, their lives were very like those described in *Lily's Dream.*

Lily, Nellie, Johanna, Harry and their friends didn't really exist, but the lives they lived and the jobs they did as servants in the Big House are as accurate as I could make them. I worked very hard at researching this book, but even so, I may have made some mistakes. Try not to judge me!

The Irish in World War One

I t might surprise you to learn that about 200,000 Irish men served in the British army during World War One. There were many reasons for this. Some, like Harry, joined up because they felt that

Imperial War Museum

Soldiers from the Royal Irish Rifles in a trench near the Somme in World War I.

protecting small nations like Belgium was the right thing to do. Some were following in the footsteps of their father or grandfather. Some went because army pay was better than anything else available to them, and some went because they thought that fighting in a war would be a great adventure.

Lots of recruits lied about their age, which was easy to do, as at the time many people didn't have birth certificates. (Sometimes, if a boy was tall enough, no questions were asked.)

Of the Irish who went to war, at least 35,000 were killed. Many returned with serious injuries that would change their lives forever. Some suffered from trauma that was not fully understood at the time.

The political situation had changed while the Irish soldiers were away, and many were shunned on their return. The 1916 Rising, which aimed to set up an independent Irish republic, had taken place during World War One, and some people believed the soldiers should have stayed at home to fight for Irish

freedom. Because of this, many ex-soldiers were secretive about their war service and died without talking about their experiences.

The Christmas Truce

Many of the soldiers who signed up to fight in 1914 believed that the war would be over by Christmas. Sadly, they were wrong, as it continued until November 1918. Like all wars, this one was horrific, and the story of the Christmas truce is one of the very few bright moments.

In December 1914, Pope Benedict XV pleaded with the leaders of both sides to allow an official truce

Neil Richardson/The O'Brien Press

This Princess Mary Tin was sent as a present to soldiers at Christmas in 1914; it contained things like chocolate and tobacco and was paid for by a public fund backed by Princess Mary.

at Christmas, but he was unsuccessful. Even so, that Christmas many little truces sprang up spontaneously across the Western Front. These truces were unofficial, and happened without any formal planning.

The opposing trenches were not far apart (sometimes only thirty metres) with an area called 'no man's land' in between. Across this space, the soldiers could hear each other talking, and smell their cooking.

On Christmas Eve 1914 it was cold, with frost and a light snowfall. The German emperor had sent Christmas trees to his troops, and on December 24th, soldiers began to set them up outside their trenches. As night fell, they sang carols and called greetings to the opposing armies.

At dawn on Christmas day, in many sections of the front, the Germans began to emerge from trenches and advance cautiously. There are some reports of men holding up signs reading 'You no shoot – we no shoot'.

Gradually they ventured further and further into no man's land, and British soldiers did the same. The

enemies, who were tired of war, began to shake hands and chat, and they exchanged small gifts.

Many of the Germans had once worked in England, so could speak English. Some soldiers exchanged addresses, though there's no evidence they ever met after the war.

Soccer was popular in both countries and there were small kick-abouts between the armies, with goals marked out by caps and helmets. It wasn't easy to play on the frozen ground, as the men were wearing heavy army boots. Where there was a ball, it was made of leather, and became very wet and soggy. The Germans always claim to have won a match 3 – 2!

When darkness fell, the soldiers returned to their own trenches, though in many places the peace held until midnight.

By the end of December, letters began to arrive home to England and Ireland, and newspapers reported what had happened. At first people didn't believe these stories, but some soldiers had cameras,

and gradually photos were published, showing the truth.

Junior officers did not stop the truces, but generals were against them, feeling that men would fight less well if they were friends with their former enemies. In the Christmases after 1914, the war continued without a break.

Further Reading

These are some of the books and websites that helped me as I was writing this book:

Maeve de Markievicz by Clive Scoular

Constance Markievicz by Anne Haverty

The Gore-Booths of Lissadell by Dermot James

Blazing a Trail by Sarah Webb and Lauren O'Neill

www.Lissadellhouse.com

www.iwm.org.uk

Acknowledgements

Thanks to my lovely family who held my hand as we wandered around this strange new pandemic world.

Thanks to all at Lissadell House for their ongoing help with the small details (my own fault if I got any of them wrong!)

Thanks to the team at O'Brien Press for another lovely production. Special thanks to my kind and patient editor, Helen.

Thanks to Rachel Corcoran for yet another lovely cover.

Thanks to my writing friends, Sarah Webb, Siobhan Mac Donald and Roisin Meaney – for the title brainstorming, and the ongoing bookish chats.

Thanks to my girls, Ellen and Annie, who talked through the plot of this book with me, and came up with some great ideas.

Thanks as always to my young readers, who have been so enthusiastic about Lily, and encouraged me to tell more of her story.